"The contribution of UI
inspirational. Anita Goyal's 'Voices from Punjab is well ——
unique in content. Perhaps one of the best portrayals of British Punjabi
success in recent history."

Asian Voice

"Anita is an inspiration for women all over the world. Her charity work
has taken her to many rural places around the globe, and now this book
has taken her into the histories of some of the most inspiring Asian
women in Britain today. Well done, Anita!"

**Sunita Arora, Philanthropist and
Director at the Arora Foundation**

"Anita Goyal is genuine and generous in her mission to create a positive
impact to the many organisations she supports.
Through the creation of this book, she is using education to promote
change, all the while championing and inspiring others. The world
needs more people like Anita Goyal."

Manika Kaur, Philanthropist and Musical Artist

"Stories have the power to teach. They allow us to learn and see the world through the eyes of many as it was, it is and could be. Through hearing the stories of our past we can build a better future, learning the lessons history has to teach us. And history has many lessons to teach; it is important that we do not forget them and keep sharing them as generations have done before us. This book continues that tradition, passing words of wisdom, warning and wonder from one generation to the next and beyond. It should serve as real life lessons for a better tomorrow."

Reena Ranger, Philanthropist and Chair of Women Empowered

"Everyone has a story to tell – it's how you tell it that matters. This book is sure to tantalise memories from times gone by, as it recognises the journey of acclimatisation that mothers, aunts and friends went through to get to the other side. Anita has taken 15 such stories and injected an energy that is sure to inspire you."

Manjit Gill, CEO of Binti International

Voices
from
Punjab

The strength and resilience of
15 Punjabi Women living in the UK

ANITA GOYAL

WITH

AASTHA K SINGHANIA

Matador
9 Priory Business Park,
Wistow Road, Kibworth Beauchamp,
Leicestershire, LE8 0RX
Tel: 0116 279 2299
Email: books@troubador.co.uk
Web: www.troubador.co.uk/matador
Twitter: @matadorbooks

ISBN 978 1838591 335

British Library Cataloguing in Publication Data.
A catalogue record for this book is available from the British Library.

Printed and bound by CPI Group (UK) Ltd, Croydon, CR0 4YY
Typeset in Minion Pro by Troubador Publishing Ltd, Leicester, UK

Matador is an imprint of Troubador Publishing Ltd

Dedicated to my many mothers

Parmjit Rai, Santosh Goyal,
Tarseem Sehmi, Sham Kaur Sehmi,
Gurcharan Kanda and Purni Devi

CONTENTS

FOREWORD

Anita Goyal and Aastha K Singhania have successfully encouraged fifteen amazing women to openly share their stories, including inspirational industry leaders such as Dr Kamel Hothi, Baroness Verma, Sarita Sabharwal, Lady Desai and Lady Noon. They also captured the stories of everyday women such as Santosh Goyal, Parmjit Rai and Kuljit Sharma, exploring the vibrancy that these women emulate through their actions and the relationship with their culture and identity.

Voices from Punjab is a collection of fifteen beautifully told stories, sharing the challenges, obstacles and successes of these Punjabi women and their families as they emigrated to the United Kingdom. Each of these women have had a huge impact on the lives of those around them, and by publishing this book they are sharing their stories with the world. This book is a true celebration of diversity, not only in the UK but also among Punjabi women, as it captures how one common location can produce such different stories and futures. The fifteen stories are woven together in a uniquely personal way, acknowledging their similarities and embracing their differences in the face of Western society and its extreme cultural demands.

I'm really proud that the Hemraj Goyal Foundation is supporting this book by giving all profits to support a livelihood project for vulnerable women in Punjab and education for young women and girls. I hope that women everywhere are inspired by *Voices from Punjab* and the purposeful difference it will make. By sharing these stories, Anita and Aastha are highlighting the sacrifice that these women have made when their lives were picked up and moved, to inspire everyone regardless of their gender, religion, age, or cultural identity.

AVNISH GOYAL

Founding Trustee of the Hemraj Goyal Foundation
Chair of Hallmark Care Homes and Chair of Care England

My Beginning

ANITA GOYAL
WITH PARMJIT RAI

My mother was the one who suggested that I would write a book
one day, after consulting the astrological chart which was made
after my birth. This was a decade ago and at the time I believed
that my mother was being facetious, laughing it off as nothing
serious. Deep down, however, I knew that this was something I
would love to pursue, though I put it on the back burner for a long
time. I have been on an incredible journey with my co-author,
Aastha, and together we started to explore the lives of women
with roots and heritage from Punjab in India. Fifteen women
were chosen to represent the true spirit of Punjabi women living
in the United Kingdom in the twenty-first century.

Punjab has suffered massively at the hands of British rule,
from exploiting its fertile land for resources, to tormenting and
killing people at the Jallianwala Bagh massacre in 1919, to forcing
innocent families to leave their settled abodes, struggling to keep
themselves alive during the Partition of India in 1947. Many Sikhs
and Hindus were a part of Western Punjab and Muslims of East
Punjab. Partition displaced many from their homes, ancestry and
the life which they had made for themselves. Families lost their
loved ones, saw their women getting raped and killed, and were
forced to travel with uncertainty, unsure as to how they would

reach the other side of the border – dead or alive. No one could be trusted on either side and many had to let go of everything they had to start afresh. The Partition Museum in Amritsar, India, has a record of many such voices which cried out for help at the time but seemed to have gone silent over the years.

Today Punjab is considered one of the wealthiest states of India, not only financially but also in spirit. Punjab is also synonymous with colour, festivities and merriment. My heritage is Punjabi and as a British-born Indian, I am fascinated with how life was so different to how it is in the United Kingdom. This is where my ancestors were from and only through my short holidays to India with my mother did I realise how important it is to connect with your roots. Upon each subsequent visit, I started to identify gaps in my knowledge about Indian history, especially in relation to the British Empire. I was educated in British schools, being born in Forest Gate in East London, and this part of history was never taught. This book is not a historical book, but an opportunity for us to emphasise the real-life stories of women with a common background – coming from Punjab to celebrate their triumphs over cultural differences and gender stereotypes in the UK.

My first-hand experience of this was being born into a Punjabi family in 1972. I will start with this first. We lived in a joint family, which was common in those days for most immigrant families. I remember a happy childhood, the youngest of three cousins and spoilt by the attention given to me by the numerous uncles, aunts and grandparents. I was described as a doll – with curly black hair, dark brown eyes and soft fair skin. Punjabi was the first language I spoke, and I am so grateful for that as when I speak this wonderful language it connects me to my culture and heritage.

My mother, Parmjit Rai, is the inspiration behind this book. She was born in 1953 in a town called Moga, which is in the state of Punjab. Moga was named after Moga Singh Gill who was a prominent person of the Gill community. Moga is recognised for its railway and it became a popular spot for travelling to Lahore (now in Pakistan). It's a city that is known for a number of educational institutions such as D.M. College and Lala Lajpat Rai Group of colleges. Many prominent people are from the district of Moga and one of them was a widely recognised Indian freedom fighter who actively participated in the Indian freedom struggle against British rule. In fact, he was one of the chief leaders of the Indian independence movement – Lala Lajpat Rai. He was born in a small village called Dhudike, which is based in the district of Moga. I mention this incredible leader for a good reason: my father, Lajpat Rai, is named after him. As a child my father would tell the story that when he was born in 1947, his uncle was in the army and he insisted that this would be the name of his newborn nephew. After Partition in 1947, Punjab was divided under East and West Punjab, purely based on Hindu and Muslim predominance in these areas. Statistics clearly show Muslim domination towards the West and Hindu domination in the East. The trouble came when the Radcliffe line was to be drawn between Amritsar and Lahore, and the decision on whether they would include Kashmir as part of India or Pakistan.

My mother studied at the S.D. College for Women in Moga, which was founded in 1969, though sadly she was discouraged from continuing with her education despite being academic. At the tender age of eighteen, in 1971, she had an arranged marriage to my father. This was the plight of many women in those days and my mother was no different. She arrived in England on a wintery cold day in January 1972, excited and naïve, looking forward to her new life in East London. Having lived a privileged life in Moga, to be immersed into a traditional family with very different values to her own was indeed a culture shock. She led a carefree and happy life in India where her every demand was met by her mother, aunties and maids. Being the only daughter out of four boisterous brothers was special for my mother as she was adored by everyone, especially her father. It was only when she was growing up that her brothers caused her to realise gender inequality. If her *chunni* ever slid off her head whilst out in public, they would challenge her about it. She takes every opportunity to remind them of that even to this day.

Can you possibly imagine what it must have been like coming to England in the 1970s to start a newly married life with a husband and family you barely know? The journey to an unknown land where it is freezing cold in the winter and rains most days? A new language to learn and an alien culture where everyone seems to know more than you? You hardly know yourself as you are just at the end of your teens, dealing with all the emotions and confusion of a new life.

My mum's first year in England was a transformational journey as she established herself as a daughter-in-law, sister-in-law and wife in a large joint family. It was tough for her as she was so young and naïve and struggled to work out who she could trust. She was only nineteen years old when she gave birth to me and was propelled into motherhood when she should have been enjoying her first year at university. It was a turning point for my mother when they celebrated my first birthday and she set about dealing with removing the *purdah* (covering the head and face with a *chunni*) together with her two sisters-in-law. She led them into removing the *chunni* completely, and the three stood united in what they believed to be an old-fashioned custom of respect. My grandfather was upset about this at first, but luckily he got over it quite quickly and accepted their decision. This custom may have worked and continued in the small village that he was from, close to Ludhiana, India, but was not appreciated in the UK.

Parmjit and Lajpat Rai (Anita's parents)

As I approached two years old, my mother was highly inspired by a female relative in Canada. Her name was Davinder. She was pretty, fair, intelligent and taught Science in a secondary school. This all happened whilst we were visiting my mother's family in Canada (her eldest brother had emigrated there in the early 1970s). Davinder could drive a car! She wore stylish Western clothes, she was educated and independent – in short, she was my mother's role model. That was all my mother needed to fight her corner and influence my father to let her eventually have driving lessons. My mother took lessons with the British School of Motoring (BSM), which was a top driving school at that time, and she passed her driving test first time round. Her reputation for being smart, determined and astute spread quickly within the local Punjabi community and it empowered other women to also start learning to drive. Others started to comment on how great it was that my mother was so smart that she could drive and it encouraged the daughters-in-law of other families to make a stand and follow in her footsteps. My mother still doesn't see how she was a leader in those days. I remind her how it must have been much harder to influence others, especially in the absence of social media. I hope that I have learnt leadership from my inspirational mother too.

In 2014, I married my incredibly supportive husband, Avnish Goyal. I'll never forget our first date, when he asked me where my mother was from. As I proceeded to tell him that my mother was born in a city called Moga in India and that he may not have heard of it, his jaw dropped, and he informed that he knew it very well – he was also born there in 1966! That was the start of our dynamic journey together. I later discovered that both my mum and husband attended the same primary school – Dev Samaj School in Moga. They were connected in the most unusual way through me – albeit at different times.

In 2016, my mother took Avnish and I to visit Sri Harmandir Sahib (the Golden Temple) in Amritsar, India, and unknown to me at the time, it was the mysterious start of my journey for this book. In 2019, I visited the Golden Temple with a group of friends and my husband with an intense desire to experience this sacred place more closely. It is a place for everyone irrespective of geographical, social, political or religious background. For a Sikh, this is a special sacred place which is beautifully situated in the middle of the holy lake like a magnificent lotus flower. As I sat wearing a light blue Punjabi suit with my head covered, I felt an intense connection with my grandparents who were also Sikh and I grew up listening to their prayers at the crack of dawn in Moga.

My mother had mentioned the Jallianwala Bagh massacre as we walked past the white marble monument of sacrifice – and this was the trigger that sparked my curiosity. The Jallianwala Bagh massacre took place on 13 April 1919. This is Baisakhi Day and it is one of the most important dates in the Sikh calendar. It is a long-established harvest festival in Punjab and this day also commemorates 1699, the year Sikhism was born. The tenth guru, Guru Gobind Singh, chose Baisakhi as the occasion to transform Sikhs into a family of soldier saints known as *Khalsa Panth*. It was on 13 April 1919 that General R.E.H. Dyer gave the order to open fire on an unarmed, peaceful crowd of men, women and children listening to speeches at Jallianwala Bagh, close to the Sri Harmandir Sahib. We visited the Jallianwala Bagh, which is now a public garden in Amritsar, and it houses a memorial of national importance, established in 1951 by the Government of India. On 13 April 2019, Avnish and I were honoured to visit the Indira Gandhi National Centre for the Arts (IGNCA) in collaboration with The Arts and Cultural Heritage Trust (TAACHT) for the inauguration of the Jallianwala Bagh Centenary. It was one thought that I shared back in 2016 about why this horrific event happened that led me on this path of inquiry. Along the way, people have entered my life to educate me further.

In 2018, I had an opportunity to meet Lady Kishwar Desai, a prominent author and Chairperson of The Arts and Cultural Heritage Trust in Amritsar, and she agreed to share her story in this book. She inspired me to learn even more about this part of our history in her chapter 'My Heritage Our Partition', with the Partition Museum in Amritsar bringing all this to life. It couldn't have come at a timelier point. Lady Desai has released her recent book, *Jallianwala Bagh, 1919: The Real Story*, to mark the centenary of this atrocity, committed against so many innocent people. It looks at how the massacre became the flame that ignited the freedom movement.

The writing of this book has inspired me to influence all my family to be part of the Partition Museum in Amritsar to support its ongoing educational work with young people. It opened its doors to the world in Amritsar on 17 August 2017 and the Punjab

Government declared this as Partition Remembrance Day. The Partition of India in 1947 was recognised as the largest migration in human history, and estimates suggest that up to 18 million people lost their homes, with a shocking 2 million losing their lives. On 14 August 1947, Pakistan celebrated Independence and Muhammad Ali Jinnah was sworn in as the first Governor-General of Pakistan. Lord Mountbatten selected 15 August 1947 as Indian Independence Day, as it is the second anniversary of Japan's surrender. On the same day, Pandit Jawaharlal Nehru was sworn in as the first Prime Minister of independent India.

Voices from Punjab is a collection of fifteen stories including highly influential Punjabi women in politics such as Baroness Sandip Verma, Lady Kishwar Desai, Lady Mohini Kent Noon and Seema Malhotra MP, UK Parliament. Although Seema is British born, she returned to explore her roots in her epic visit to Punjab when she was eighteen years old, where she discovered the beauty of her culture and love for India. Seema is the first female Punjabi Member of the House of Commons, and she understands the demand to raise awareness of ethnic communities in the UK. She uses her passion and her position as a platform to share the issues of the Hindu population with the rest of Parliament.

Baroness Sandip Verma shares the beautiful story of how her husband has been her biggest champion and supporter throughout her career. Sandip left me inspired; her energy and passion is so contagious and I admire her for standing up to the gender inequality that exists in our world today. Her greatest accomplishment is her recent position as Chair of United Nations (UN) Women UK.

My co-author, Aastha K Singhania, and I have endeavoured to capture the experiences and impact of the Partition of India in 1947 through Kuljit Sharma, Raj Nayyar and Santosh Goyal's stories. These women were born in the 1930s before Partition and they all had contrasting experiences of being raised in India, but almost identical lives when they arrived in the UK. Kuljit was raised dressed as a boy in her early years and had a privileged life, well educated by her father who was a consolidation officer and believed in gender equality. Santosh was not exposed to a formal education, but her father taught her a lot about Ayurvedic medicine and other remedies. Raj Nayyar, in her chapter 'Iron Lady', lived in Lahore and was known in her college as a 'lioness'! She was an ardent admirer of Mahatma Gandhi and had the honour of meeting him quite unexpectedly in his ashram in Bangladesh.

Lady Mohini Kent Noon shares in her chapter 'Witness to a Life' the heartbreaking story of a family leaving Pakistan to take the train to India on a journey with atrocious violence and killings of innocent men and women. Mohini gives us an insight into her dynamic life as a filmmaker, journalist and author of many books such as *Black Taj*, a captivating novel which sensitively explores the effects of Partition and social unrest, resentment and religious conflict in 1947 India; her riveting story about her grandmother who found herself in *purdah* (the practice of screening women from men literally by a curtain) after marriage; and the commendable charity work to which Mohini has dedicated so much of her life. The charity that Lady Noon leads – LILY Against Human Trafficking – is close to my heart. She has inspired the next generation in fundraising for the incredible projects that support women and girls in India that have been trafficked.

The Hemraj Goyal Foundation (HGF) has committed funding to work with some phenomenal NGOs (non-governmental organisations) against human trafficking through prevention, rescue and rehabilitation, helping survivors lead free, healthy and fulfilling lives. The Hemraj Goyal Foundation was set up in memory of my father-in-law and was created in 2010 by my husband, Avnish Goyal. Hemraj Goyal arrived in the UK from Moga (Punjab) forty-nine years ago with the vision of a better life for his family. This vision, as well as his hard work and determination, has inspired not only his children but his grandchildren, friends and extended family to have boundless ambition. The growth of the foundation has led to HGF being an established and recognised charity in the public field. It is our mission to encourage the next generation to engage in philanthropy at all levels.

The stories in *Voices from Punjab* are balanced with everyday women such as Santosh Goyal, wife of the late Hemraj Goyal, who the foundation is named after, and the sacrifices that they have made to allow the next generation to flourish and thrive. Santosh is also my mother-in-law and these last few years I have had the privilege, together with my husband Avnish, to serve her with kindness and compassion in her twilight years. I am grateful for the values that she has instilled in my husband so that he can be the best possible husband to me and the greatest father to our children, Anand, Simran and Simran.

Suffering from depression dominated a large part of Mani's life. In her chapter 'Unknown Land, Unknown Life', Mani shares how she lifted herself out of her sorrow to start the charity Billion Women. It was set up to champion the rights of women made homeless, by empowering them to find a voice.

Dr Kamel Hothi OBE shares her challenging journey from cashier to a director in banking in her chapter 'Two Worlds'. Kamel has experienced first-hand the struggles of smashing glass ceilings, discrimination and gender imbalance across the banking sector over four decades. She is now ranked in the top one hundred most influential black, Asian and minority ethnic leaders in the UK and was awarded an OBE for services to promoting diversity in banking. In 2017, after thirty-eight years she retired to support several boards as a non-executive director, adviser and trustee, including on the Queen's Commonwealth Trust, whilst still balancing the demands of a traditional Indian extended family with four generations living in one household. Kamel is a compassionate woman who is influencing the charitable sector in a huge way, with her coherent vision for the Alzheimer's Society, gradually leading the way for change in the South Asian community. Her story is compelling and encourages women to embrace the opportunities that may come their way.

The personal life of Rita Chowdhry is shared with compassion and shows her ambition to strive for a better life following the death of her father when she was just nine years old. The wonderful values that her mother and father instilled in her resonate with all that she stands for. Her family are the centre of her world and they are such a talented household. In 2018, her daughter Leah swam the English Channel from England to France in a staggering fourteen hours and forty-four minutes. Through her vision, Rita has created a business on coaching and consultancy for businesses and individuals who feel they want to fulfil their potential in their professional or personal lives, and as a result she has received multiple awards for her business acumen.

Some of the women in this book have engaged in radio and TV work, such as Sarita Sabharwal and Rajni Kaul. The life story of Sarita Sabharwal, the winner of the best radio show and best presenter of Spectrum Radio and TV Asia, is shared in her chapter 'The Show Must Go On'. The beautiful voice of Sarita on Sunrise Radio has entertained many over the years and she is well known for hosting the popular drive-time show now on Lyca Radio's *Dil Se*. She shares her memorable interview with

Benazir Bhutto. (Benazir Bhutto was a Pakistani politician who served as Prime Minister of Pakistan from 1988 to 1990 and again from 1993 to 1996. She was the first woman to head a democratic government in a Muslim majority nation.)

Dr Mandeep Rai has the chutzpah that Punjabi journalists are known for, and in her chapter 'Creative Vision' she shares her family story and heritage from Punjab. Her experience as a BBC World Service journalist in creative activism and development, reporting from over a hundred countries, allowed her to gain deep insights into the culture and values of global communities. Her ethnicity and leadership qualities have helped her to gain trust and acceptance from all kinds of people, cutting across cultures and classes, and allowing worldwide access to unique insights and life lessons.

Rajni Kaul was the woman behind her husband's success in the BBC programme *Nai Zindagi Naya Jeevan*, which was the first major programme targeted at Hindi- and Urdu-speaking viewers. She ventured into the hospitality industry and started the famous Indian restaurant, Gaylord, in London. This was the Asian venue to be seen at back in those days, and many eminent personalities dined there, including Margaret Thatcher. Rajni had an opportunity to become a producer and broadcaster at BBC Radio in the 1970s; she embraced this new opportunity having worked at All India Radio in the 1940s in India. Her story has so many powerful messages of strength and determination.

The heartbreaking story of Kalbir Bains shares how she married into a patriarchal Punjabi family and had to have an abortion. Her chapter 'Always "Our Daughter"' shares her painful experience of being denied motherhood by her husband, and provides insight into how her life experience has spurred her to write her own book, *Not Our Daughter*, which is her true story of life as a daughter-in-law.

These women are champions and leaders of their own lives and they openly share how they have overcome adversities of culture, financial hardship, dowry abuse and *purdah*. They explain the complexities of dual identities and balancing careers with family life. They have embraced British life, either through arranged marriages in Punjab or growing up in the UK in the 1960s and '70s, breaking through language barriers, racism and gender inequality to become the women they are today.

Parmjit with Anita (mother and daughter)

Simran Goyal, Anita Goyal, Avnish Goyal, Santosh Goyal,
Anand Goyal, Sabrina Pervez, Simran Sehmi

ONE

My Heritage Our Partition
LADY KISHWAR DESAI

Elegant, chic and stylish, Kishwar Desai is a writer, former journalist and editor, a philanthropist and a leader – a Lady with a vision. She is a wonderful mother to her son and daughter and the wife of Meghnad Jagdishchandra Desai, Baron Desai – a British economist and Labour politician. Kishwar is also Chair of The Arts and Cultural Heritage Trust (TAACHT) which has just set up the world's first Partition Museum at Town Hall, Amritsar, Punjab, India. There is so much we can learn from Kishwar through her award-winning novels and columns that reveal the atrocities committed against women in India. Her latest book is based on the hidden history of a massacre: *Jallianwala Bagh, 1919: The Real Story*.

ANITA GOYAL

Most of us remember our childhood only when there is some despair or despondency involved in our memories. Fortunately, I don't remember much of mine, which in itself is a positive sign. My name is Kishwar Desai and I was born in Ambala in 1956 into a family who were eager to have a girl child amongst them. I would think of them to be quite progressive for their time because it was very unusual to hear of parents longing to have a girl as their progeny.

My father was a very honest police officer who refused to bow down to the minimal demands of senior politicians or of high-ranking officers. As a result, he was posted around to different cities and we moved a lot with him. A lot of my character building came from inhaling the different vibes and cultures of these places, also becoming more adaptable by adjusting to any situation I was put into. Having – or not having – luxury comforts never really bothered me. People still see me as an easy-going person, but are shocked and surprised when they read my books, which deal with really dark subjects, revealing a different side to my personality that they did not know. Even as a journalist, it is important to stand face to face with harsh realities in order to speak about them and I believe that has changed my course of both thinking and writing.

My childhood was very different to what most children go through today. The only source of entertainment today seems to be video games or some other form of technology that was not accessible when I was growing up. We mostly spent our time reading and writing, which enhanced our creative flow of thought and made us more knowledgeable about the world around us. I was a voracious reader and could pick up five books of different genres and read them all at the same time. I would keep a diary and note down day-to-day anecdotes to keep me busy, inspiring me to write. When I grew up, I was amazed to find these synopses of stories that I had written very early on, which I developed to become drafts of the type of narratives I wanted to later explore.

As a child, I was surrounded by stories of 1947 and the Partition of India into two countries. In 1964, my father, who was in the Border Security Force, was posted in Ferozepur, Punjab. That year we were also at war with Pakistan. Every night, we could hear the airplanes flying over our houses, or hear the sirens go off, which would mean hiding in our bunkers. When the situation got worse, my mother felt that the city was no longer safe to be in. We decided to move to Ambala, which was considerably safer, and we packed four or five people into a Fiat, which my mother drove, taking us to Ambala and my grandparents' house. That same night she returned to Ferozepur to be with my father and, coincidently enough, Ambala got bombed that same night. The bombs fell very close to our house and we all had to hide under the beds. I was scared and as an eight-year-old I always used to plead with my mother to never leave me behind if there was an attack. Incidents like this may have fuelled my imagination and I often wonder what it was like when people had to move with their families from Pakistan to India or vice versa, and what they must have gone through after losing everything they ever had – belongings and loved ones alike.

Partition has always been a talking point amongst people around me, especially for the people of Punjab. The land of Punjab has suffered so much. All the glitz and charm this state is known for hides the tragedies that their families have endured. My maternal grandparents moved from Lahore when riots broke out; they felt that the place was no longer safe for them and their three daughters. Lahore, my mother tells me, was a very cosmopolitan city, with so much culture, glamour and cinema, also known as 'the Paris of the East'. My grandfather was in denial, because no one really believed that the land would get divided in such a brutal way. To calm my grandmother, he indulged her fears and packed one suitcase to drive down and stay with relatives in Amritsar. Little did they know, but this trip would plant them on Indian soil for generations to come.

They couldn't go back and my grandmother lost everything, from furniture down to the last teaspoon. They had to start all over again and, like others in the same situation, had to resettle themselves into a new life. My grandfather did go back once and was surprised to see that someone had already moved into their house. He couldn't bring back too many things but made sure he packed all his books and a few odd bits here and there. Life had changed completely, and it was time to find a foothold in settling in. They practised patience and made sure their anxieties did not come through. Like others, my grandparents also maintained their dignity in front of their children, as they did not want to distress them. Parents had to maintain dignity as an important part of parenthood. As a result, the children did not realise what had happened and it was only later that my mother, who was a young child of thirteen at the time, understood the gravity of the situation.

Despite their individual loss and suffering, the people retained their idealism. They were inspired by their leaders, especially Mahatma Gandhi. They had all seen the freedom struggle and were proud to be acting for the welfare of the country. The idea of independence overshadowed their grief and therefore not many of them speak about it. As a result of this, so the world doesn't either. There are so many unrecorded incidents, and lives unaccounted for – girls who just disappeared one day and were never spoken about or people who stayed back in Pakistan and changed their religion. The Partition Museum brings back those memories, and we are still trying to record and archive every emotion, torment or suffering that people at the time may have gone through.

Since my childhood, I've shown a very creative outlook on life and career and knew that I wanted to see myself grow as either a writer or a journalist. I have worked for private media organisations, from being a production controller to an anchor; I worked in all aspects of media, and rose to the top of my profession, eventually setting up and running a TV channel. I feel lucky to have had the opportunity to anchor breakfast shows at TV Today and women's shows at Doordarshan. Initially, I was very pleased with my progress and the work I was contributing, but with time I realised that the English channels were too elitist and that we, as journalists, were neglecting content production in Hindi. After working for Hindi channels, I felt the same about Punjabi content and realised that whatever I did, subconsciously, I would return to Punjab to make a difference. I set up a Punjabi regional channel, and I made sure that the channel was not only about Gurbaani or Punjabi pop songs, but also Punjabi literature from authors like Amrita Pritam, folklore and stories of interest to the region. To reinstate the glory of Punjab, notable directors like Mahesh Bhatt helped us shoot short Punjabi films, which we would air on our channel. Today, I can proudly say that I made a difference and gave excellent programming content whilst working in television.

With time, lots of things change. The media industry was not what it was when I joined. 'Commercial' was the way forward and my heart was no longer in it. By then my children had grown up too and were studying abroad. I had moved to publishing, which was more serious and gave me the insight to this side of writing, which I enjoyed. Things were not only changing with my career but also on the private front. Up until then, I had been married to my husband for almost twenty-five years but soon realised that we both wanted to move on. Sometimes, a marriage does not mean that one needs to stay with one another even when there is a conflict of interest. I have two beautiful children out of this wedlock but after so many years we were both leading separate lives. Fortunately, this decision was mutual and we were separated for a little period of time. Within this period, I got to edit a book, which my present husband, Meghnad Desai, had written on the famous Indian Bollywood actor, Dilip Kumar. I had met him before that but got to meet him a couple of times while I was working on this project. It was in these meetings that Meghnad decided that he wanted to spend the rest of his life with me, he tried really hard to persuade me and eventually I realised that he was right!

The most traumatic time comes in a woman's life when you are trying to do the right thing, without breaking the hearts of your loved ones. To marry Meghnad was a decision that I couldn't take alone. I sat my son and daughter down and asked for their permission and discussed what they felt about him. My son, being a complete renaissance man, acted with such maturity and sensibility that I got my strength to take this step. My daughter too was very understanding, and she flew over to London to support our marriage. There is so much that a woman goes through at a time like this that it becomes very difficult to know which way life will take you. One sits down in retrospection, questioning yourself whether it is you who is demanding more of life or if you are capable of putting in a little more effort and staying in the marriage so as not to affect your children and people around you. However, it was a collaborative effort from my children and parents, who gave me so much support, that helped Meghnad and me start a new life together. Meghnad, too, came in person to ask for my hand in marriage, and it seemed like everyone was trying their best in their own way to do the right thing.

I moved to the United Kingdom almost sixteen years ago and have been very pleasantly surprised to see the warmth with which his friends received me. The country has welcomed me. Being with Meghnad has kept me intellectually stimulated, be it in conversation with him or accompanying him to the House of Lords, listening to great debates from great minds from across the globe. It has been a different world and I am excited to see myself becoming a part of it. When one is fairly progressive and liberal, you can fit in beautifully like the missing piece of a puzzle. It was in the UK that I received the Costa Award for my first novel, *Witness the Night*, which dwelt on the issues of female foeticide, set in a small village in Jalandhar, Punjab. Only then did I realise that there is enormous scope in Britain because it is open to different ideas and more cosmopolitan writing. With my books I have travelled across the UK and countries in Europe, and even all the way to Australia, to speak to audiences who relate to the subject, and who have communicated their apprehensions or experience to me. Novel writing is not limited to one genre or area; it explores universalities which are accepted by people all across the world.

People and institutions in the UK have also been so very generous in helping bring forth the Partition Museum with the kind of vision with which I set it up. History is mostly written to capture the essence of the time from the rulers' perspective, with museums encapsulating their lifestyles, war stories, weapons and the kingdom they built. Very rarely do we see what the people of that time went through, their joys and troubles. I wanted to bring to the forefront not the stories of leaders – such as Gandhi, Nehru or Jinnah, which are often documented for people to see – but of the ordinary people who have suffered. I formed The Arts and Cultural Heritage Trust in India, initially with our own money, and then started getting donations from friends and family, allowing us to set up the world's first partition museum in Amritsar. The museum is housed in the historic Town Hall, which was allotted to our trust by the Punjab Government, for which we are very grateful. The museum has been built entirely through donations – of money, memorabilia and, most importantly, memories. We have a large ongoing programme of building archives and recorded oral histories to understand what the impact was on the people who were being divided and forced to migrate. The British took most of the official documents, pre-1947, which are actually a part of Indian history and would prove helpful in research. This meant that we had to go around the country and accumulate anything that was associated with Partition and could be kept in the museum. Institutions and people have therefore been very supportive in helping us identify what could be useful and, in many cases, sharing the documents with us. It is in this manner that we managed to acquire artefacts, photographs and documents which were required to create the museum. These archives are not only in Britain, but have spread all across the globe with people migrating to Africa, or America or other parts of the world, taking with them any letters, private or public papers and photographs. The work is immense and my vision is even bigger. We have a very small window of time as most people are now no longer with us and we have to act rather quickly to get what we can.

There is so much that we women want to achieve in our lives. Thank God for our 'multi-tasking' skills that allow us to be able to juggle and perform so beautifully at every stage. My husband has always been very supportive, but guilt has always been a part of me. No matter how hard I tried, I would always feel guilty about neglecting something at some point. But that is inevitable. One has to make adjustments and so do people around you. When my daughter was young, I once forgot to pick her up after her tennis class. I panicked and found her sitting all by herself, tearful and upset. I felt terrible and kept apologising. But today when I reflect on instances like this, I have learnt how important it was to forgive myself. As a mother and as a woman, I had tried my best and it's only human for me to falter at some step. We have to be kind to ourselves and not let these slip-ups dim the energy and fire we possess.

No matter how old you are you can always go back to doing what you love. I wrote my first book at fifty, because I knew this is what I had always wanted to do. I have been a seeker all my life. A seeker for meaning and for learning. Life is a constant challenge for everyone and all I know is that one shouldn't do the same thing over and over again. There is no learning in that. Push your horizons and you will be amazed at how much life has to offer each one of us. There was a quote which was stuck to my mirror when I was a teenager, and it was the last thing I would read before going to sleep. It helped me keep the fire ignited and passion burning for all that I wanted to achieve. I hope it helps you in the same way.

> *Do not go gentle into that good night,*
> *Rage, rage against the dying of the light.*
>   Dylan Thomas

Unveiling of the Gandhi Statue in Parliament Square

*Amitabh Bachchan (left), Shweta Bachchan (centre) with Kishwar Desai (right)
at the launch of the Gandhi statue*

*On stage for the launch of the Gandhi statue with David Cameron,
Lord Desai and Amitabh Bachchan*

*Opening of the Partition Museum in 2017 top far right, Lord Desai and Lady
Desai; bottom left, Mallika Ahluwalia, CEO, curator and co-founder of the
world's first partition museum*

With Gurinder Chadha and Indian actress Huma Qureshi

Two

Two Worlds

Dr Kamel Hothi OBE

Ranked within the top one hundred most influential black, Asian and minority ethnic leaders in the UK, Dr Kamel Hothi OBE is adviser to several organisations such as the Queen's Commonwealth Trust Fund. Kamel has been breaking glass ceilings in the banking world for over four decades, from cashier to director, strategist and architect of numerous programmes and initiatives that have changed the shape of the banking industry.

Receiving an honorary doctorate from the World Sikh University and being appointed an officer of the Order of the British Empire (OBE) for services to promoting diversity in banking – this is the professional life of the dynamic Dr Kamel Hothi OBE.

Kamel's personal life is a mirror image of the dynamism that she has displayed for over four decades in the corporate world. This is the untold story of an inspirational woman which will leave you even more moved by her achievements in the face of all the odds that were stacked against her.

Anita Goyal

I think when you've been uprooted once and you've lost everything, the second home is easier to leave behind. Imagine taking your young family into an unknown land, filled with trepidation and uncertainty. That emotional and physical trauma was inflicted on so many people at that time – the Partition of India. My family were Sikh, fleeing Pakistan to settle in Punjab; thankfully my parents survived the Partition of India – the biggest migration of refugees which eventually brought us here to the United Kingdom to build a better life.

My mother was a very beautiful and kind woman inside and out. She spoke of how my father had protected her on the walk from Pakistan to India. He dressed her up in men's trousers and a turban so as to disguise her striking good looks in order to avoid being kidnapped or abused. This was the story of so many that took the refugee walk in 1947. Families did what they thought was right to protect the honour of their women.

I was born in 1963 in a small town called Kang Saboo, located in Jalandhar, Punjab. I'm the youngest of six, with three brothers and two sisters. My family had to start from scratch as there was little money in Punjab, particularly in our small village. My father was a civil engineer and would spend two years away at a time building the Bhakra Dam, the largest of its time. This impressive structure is a concrete gravity dam, which stretches across the Sutlej River, near the border of Punjab and Himachal Pradesh in northern India. It is used primarily to produce hydroelectricity. It was a long-term project that stemmed over several years and while my dad was away at work, we lived with our uncle and aunt in the family house in Kang Saboo, farming the land.

My eldest sister was soon married and went to live with her husband and his family in London, England, in a town called Slough. She sponsored my father to come over to England in the 1960s to find work post the call from the British Government during the Windrush era. My mother was left in Punjab, yet again, to take care of the family. For a woman who had never stepped out of her village, she handled this remarkably well. She was incredibly brave when my father eventually invited us over. She brought my four siblings and I to England in 1969 – I was just six years old. There is quite an age gap between my siblings and I, but despite this, my mother got us all through the airport system in a foreign land without speaking a word of English. The interrogation my brother Avtar had to endure at the UK Border Control was quite stressful, and in conjunction with the huge language barrier it all made for a deeply daunting experience. I remember arriving at Heathrow and I'd forgotten what my father looked like. I hadn't seen him for a couple of years. I must have been four years old when he left India. My mother pointed my father out and I ran and grabbed his legs. I remember him sweeping me up in his arms and holding me close. The immigration officers, however, were just seconds behind. They ran over, they tried to *literally* pull us apart. My father got very defensive and he shouted, "She's my daughter! Leave her alone!" I think that's the first time I remember him openly showing me love.

We moved in with my sister and her in-laws and extended family in their home in Slough. There were around twelve of us living in a three-bedroom house. It was a setup that most Indians were confronted with when arriving in the UK with very little. Life was bleak and very simple in the 1960s and '70s, and most Indians sought employment as labourers. My brothers all acquired jobs in factories and worked very hard. My brother Avtar (fifth in line) did well as an apprentice at Mars chocolate factory. Most women also found work in factories like Burton's Biscuits. Some may know these incredibly tasty biscuits such as Maryland Cookies, Jammie Dodgers and Wagon Wheels!

Unfortunately, my father developed a chip on his shoulder regarding this job, as back in India he was an eminent civil engineer and a very proud man. To keep his success alive, as much as his spirit, he'd habitually tell the story of building the almighty Bhakra Dam. My father would tell of how the President of India, Jawaharlal Nehru himself, came and admired what they had built. Sadly, when my father came to England, the only job he could get was in a factory making ice skates. There was so much discrimination around at that time and in spite of his intelligence and talents, my father didn't speak English, which became a huge barrier for him and all of us. There was little understanding of diversity and almost no concept of equality as we know it today. So the aim of most immigrants was to make enough money to return home and build better lives on our farmland. I think many like my father who showed some determination and entrepreneurial drive travelled to these shores to improve their economic wealth. Those who remained were left to farm the lands but looked across the shores to those who had flown the motherland to help furnish their needs by transmitting funds back home. I wish we had had the courage to stay there and do something to help change our homeland as it had so much to offer. Unfortunately, the sorry state now only encourages drugs and alcohol, as the next generation see no future in farming. I wish I could go back and help the youth to appreciate what riches they have at their feet and the opportunities of earning from the fruits of their land to feed the largest population on earth.

In contrast to these plush green fields, it was very different here in the UK when we came in the late 1960s. In 1968, Enoch Powell, the Conservative MP for Wolverhampton South West, delivered his infamous speech 'Rivers of Blood' opposing immigration throughout the UK.

It was a time when racism and prejudice were rife and we happened to live right in the eye of that toxic environment. My father and brothers all wore turbans when we first came to England. Naturally, they were bullied and harassed for it, almost daily. I will never forget the day when my father took my brothers to the barber's to cut their hair short! When they came home, the pain and sadness that I witnessed on my mother's face was heartbreaking. It was something to the effect of, *Oh my God, what have I done? Where have we come? How much am I willing to change, to give up for this land that is not as promised? Do I really want this?* She cherished being a Sikh, as she did her sons' uncut hair. I recall my middle brother Charanjit's healthy, glossy hair, which would shine as my mother brushed it in the sun. Uncut hair covered by a turban gives Sikhs a unique identity; a physical appearance signifying discipline and spirituality.

It was all there, the pain and hurt in her eyes, and as a woman, I think it was the first time she felt she had no voice. Keep your head bowed and do what is required to keep the peace. Watching her in her silence, sinking into her sadness and loss was a pivotal moment for me, and I think that conditioned me to become the woman I am.

My first days of school were a nightmare. I didn't have any Western clothes to wear so my sister took us to a fabric shop and bought this polyester fabric; coming from India bright colours were naturally selected. Oranges, pinks and turquoise were the choice and she made me a pair of trousers and a little jacket, with matching ribbons for my hair. *Great job*, she thought! However, combine these bold fashion choices with the fact that I didn't speak a word of English and you might as well have pinned a sign on my head that said, 'Please, bully me'. The discrimination and isolation just became a normal way of life.

That was not to last, however. I actively adjusted, making new friends and learning how to speak English. I was good at sports and when I reached secondary school, much to my surprise and elation, I was voted head girl for sports! The memory is so vivid, I don't think I'll ever forget it. Everyone voted and I remember thinking, *Oh my God… it's me, how can it be?* All these girls had chosen me to be their leader. It was a huge responsibility but the only person I shared it with was my brother who also loved sports, as I knew the rest would not understand this concept. This was made evident one day when I came home from school one afternoon because I'd forgotten my trainers. I was wearing my PE (physical education) skirt, which was quite short, and which I had forgotten to change. I had run all the way home to get my trainers and, by chance, the first person I met when I got there was my eldest brother. He took one look at me and then delivered one hard slap to the back of my legs. He was very old-fashioned that way. I guess, in this context, old-fashioned means abusive. He shouted in such an aggressive manner to my mother and sisters that, "If I ever see her legs again, I will cut them off!" He had tuberculosis (TB) for a long time. He kept it to himself and I was so scared of him; I knew he was troubled and probably felt sad. I forgave him for that as in his mind females should not show any flesh regardless of age.

Being the youngest of six as well as having a number of nephews and nieces around me (some of similar age to me) I often felt lost in my crowded home, but at school I was an individual and a leader. I completed my secondary school education and received nothing short of outstanding results in my 'O' levels. I had started to dream of being a paediatrician or a nurse. As the final days loomed before leaving secondary school and submitting applications for higher education, I approached my father about my aspirations. To my utter disappointment he just said no: "No, you're not going anywhere. If you want to go to work then you can go to the factory with your sisters-in-law."

He then took the opportunity to remind me that he intended to marry me off, therefore there was no point! His own experiences of lack of fairness in the job market left him disillusioned. He believed that no matter how educated you were, people that looked like us would never get a chance: "You'll end up just working in a factory." This country had refused to acknowledge his qualifications or expertise, so he, in turn, was trying to prepare me for the same fate and not waste my time in getting any further qualifications. At the time I couldn't understand this. What really upset me was that I had my heart set on this path and had every intention of following it through. But he just said no.

My brother Avtar stepped in to support me. He asked my father to compromise and rather than working in a factory asked if he would allow me to find an office job. It wasn't my dream to work behind a desk, I wanted to be more practical, but this wasn't the time to argue. Avtar brought me a variety of application forms and one of them was for a cashier at TSB Bank. I applied and, at that time, there were 300 people being interviewed. I attended the interview and to everyone's surprise, I got the job! My father couldn't believe it! I didn't blame him, I could barely believe it myself.

The first week of my job was spent doing some tests in Reading (a large town on the Thames and Kennet rivers in southern England). Even then, my dad wouldn't let me go on the train by myself. My other brother, Charanjit, offered to drop me back and forth just so that I could sit these exams. I will always be grateful for the support my brothers gave me in the early years of my career. I was just sixteen.

I think that was my happiest time during those eighteen months as I also went back to Punjab for the first time for a holiday with my parents. The village and way of life were so alien to me but I loved the warm welcome and hearing all the old stories of the past, filling the gaps in my heritage. However, the trip soon highlighted a series of embarrassing and somewhat comical events. The first was when I was washing my hair with a super-foaming shampoo. The bubbles washed down the drain. I thought nothing of it until I went outside. I was embarrassed to find the huge mass of bubbles still sitting in the open drain and the whole gully was covered with foam and the women picking up their *salwars* to pass! *Why wasn't the foam draining?* But then I took a closer look at the gully; the answer was obvious. Everyone had been throwing their rubbish into the gully and the clutter was preventing the water from draining away. So, without much thought I pulled up my *salwar kameez* (Indian dress with trousers) and decided that I was going to clean it. I grabbed a broom from indoors and started to clear the gully. The people around me were laughing at first and I could hear them saying to each other, "Are you sure she's from England?" So, I challenged them: "Why are you so blind, you're living here! Why aren't you cleaning it up?" To my surprise, the resounding response seemed to be something to the effect of, "Yeah, actually, why aren't we?" And suddenly, people living in the village united and helped me clean up this little gully, trying to get the rubbish out so my shampoo suds could flow away! That's when I first recognised what it felt like to be in control and be a leader and influence others to enrol in a common mission.

I wished I had spent more time with my parents in Punjab as they were probably the happiest days I had spent with them. A year later back in the UK my life changed forever as I returned home from work to find my family getting ready to meet a young man and his family who had been introduced to my father. Two hours later they returned having said yes on my behalf to marriage, and three months later I was married to one of three brothers, all living together with their wives and parents. As custom directed, my eldest sister accompanied me as a chaperone to help me settle in for the first evening. I recall waking up in a stranger's home the following morning; as my sister and I tentatively walked down the stairs we encountered a man talking to my father-in-law. "I thought you said he only had two brothers," said my sister. "Who is he?" "I don't know," I replied, only to realise that it was my husband, who had removed his turban which he had only worn for the wedding, shaved his beard and was ready to go to work! This surreal experience continued as I remember our wedding night; it's kind of a funny story. Here was this stranger, my husband, and all my visualisation of wedding nights were from watching Bollywood films where the male would romance the new bride by singing some romantic song. So, I was imagining this in my head thinking, *He's going to start singing a romantic song to me in a minute.* However, the opposite was true: instead, my new husband pulls out this chart showing a five-year plan. He'd drawn a timeline indicating key milestones: "This is where I want to be in five years!" He spent most of the night walking through his vision and aspirations as well as the family tree and who was who. Including how he wanted me to behave: "Even if you have to act like a servant that is how it will be." I sheepishly admit that this somewhat dashed my dreams. I remember thinking, *What have I got myself into?* We still have that plan, to this day. At the time it was a little difficult for me to understand but over time it's become a platform for us to plan our future.

My married life has faced many challenges, from having a strong mother-in-law leading a large family, to living in a joint family where everyone had such varied values and beliefs. I soon learnt that my home life had to be separated from my professional life as they didn't value or appreciate my career or my business acumen. Even though I was doing well in my professional life, I was fully aware that my role at home was more important, and as long as I understood my priority in ensuring that domestic chores assigned to me were completed on time, then I would be satisfied. The juggling of these roles was best explained by my father-in-law who was my only ally in the house. He said to never share my career life with the women at home if I wanted to continue working. He recommended keeping these two worlds separate and not to let one into the other. So, I led a double life: my banking world required me to be this strong 'masculine' female with a deep voice and stern demanding looks, but at home I was a subservient wife and daughter-in-law with quiet mouse-like behaviours. I often felt like Wonder Woman changing my costumes and mannerisms to survive both worlds.

My mother had taught me well on the role of a wife and responsibilities as a daughter-in-law. "This is your main duty, caring for your in-laws," she would say and, "Keep your issues to yourself and don't complain to your husband or bring your problems to your brothers' doorstep now that you are married." In her generation she had been brought up thinking this was the role of a wife. It was difficult not being able to share any concerns or worries that I had during those dark years with anyone. However, I think my mother knew, even though we never exchanged a word. Her beautiful gentle smile would give me great comfort. She had suffered a lot over the years with a stroke that then turned into epileptic fits which would result from any stressful situation. I had become her main carer whilst I was single, and post-marriage I avoided upsetting her. I actually worried more about her wellbeing than my own, and when she passed away I was just thirty-four years old. It was one of the most heartbreaking things I had ever gone through and it took me a long time to come to terms with her loss as I really felt the true meaning of unconditional love. Soon after my mother died, my father deteriorated rapidly. He developed prostate cancer, which we discovered late and we were told he only had six weeks to live.

My father's death created so many wounds amongst my siblings, which to this day have not healed and have caused rifts between us all. Unfortunately, during these difficult times my only other ally, my father-in-law, also passed away leaving a huge hole in my life and absence of a protective figure in my maternal home. Those years were definitely the most stressful and challenging for me as I adapted to feeling alone and realising I had become an orphan. To avoid the heartache, I put all my energy and drive into my career, which helped me to focus on areas of my life that I could control and where my voice and hard work had some impact. From a cashier role I became the first Asian bank manager after doing my exams in the night whilst everyone slept. Customers in my first branch of Walton-on-Thames found it strange seeing a woman, let alone one that was Asian, as their manager, but I soon learnt how to be resilient to their sarcastic remarks and eventually won them over. I continued to work hard and after a number of years was controlling 160 branches. However, change is always inevitable, as they say, and soon Lloyds and TSB merged and I found out I was being made redundant. During this period an MD, Paul Baker – who was head of Group Operations for Lloyds TSB – had heard about one of the initiatives which I had implemented across my 160 branches resulting in some excellent results. He promptly came down to see me, leaving his business card behind. When I found out I was being made redundant I called him and he said, "Right, come to Head Office, I have a job for you!", and asked me to implement my idea across the whole group. Suddenly, I was catapulted into this new engine of the bank, which was daunting but exciting at the same time.

However, I recall walking into our head office for the first time to see a sea of white male faces staring back at me. It was the first time I felt the colour of my skin and my gender. Soon my voice became quieter amongst these strong dominating men, my suggestions overshadowed or stolen. I found it quite confusing compared to my previous role in retail branches where there was diversity amongst the staff. It only later dawned on me that this was because they were junior roles and hardly in senior management. This led me to form the Ethnic Minority Network and Women's Network with a few colleagues who also felt like I did. Our collaboration helped us understand the barriers and lack of diversity and cultural appreciation. This vocational network helped me identify how others were taking advantage of me, and so I started speaking out about these issues. Soon I was being asked to speak at other major platforms, resulting in my being invited by the Government to lead a task force to help them improve their supplier diversity, as they wanted to pitch for the Olympic Games in an attempt to improve small minority businesses' share in the contracts. Eighteen months later this White Paper helped numerous divisions across Whitehall and was one of the factors in the 2012 Games being won by London.

The new-found confidence I had gained via these volunteering roles soon pushed me to request that the bank take on my idea around how to engage Asian businesses. Asians had felt for decades that access to finance was difficult and I knew how we could fill that gap. I enrolled the board and in turn it allowed me to lead a team to develop the strategy. Four years later, we were leaders in the market. The changes we made were all done through very ethical and respectful means, having created award platforms to raise the profile of inspirational Asian business leaders as well as our bank's brand. The Asian Jewel Awards, Asian Women of Achievement Awards and Sindhi & Lohana community all benefited from my sponsorships. After thirty-odd national events it all came to an end in 2008 when the banking crisis hit. I found myself alone once again as the whole management board was asked to step down. However, they approached me to see if I could help the group regain its trust with customers and pride amongst colleagues and help steer the bank back into profit. I feel proud to say that after six years of hard work I reshaped the way we engaged with charities, transitioned our approach to volunteering across 85,000 colleagues, and led the Lloyds Bank 250th anniversary – all assisting the group back into private ownership and improving pride and trust.

In 2017, I decided to retire and invest my energies into supporting charities, becoming an adviser and trustee to the likes of the Queen's Commonwealth Trust, Teenage Cancer Trust and Alzheimer's Society to name a few, as well as a non-executive director for TLC Lions and Sterling Media. The icing on the cake was meeting the Queen, who awarded me the OBE for my years of work in improving diversity.

As my career trajectory continued to grow so did my family. Years of hardship and struggle and encountering numerous challenges along the way, which at times were so bleak, had left me with some very dark thoughts. However, my faith in God and love for my children gave me the courage and resilience to continue.

Decades later, both my sons are married and my beautiful daughters-in-law decided to live with us, each recently blessing us with three grandsons (one set of twin boys). I'm also proud to say I kept my promise of thirty-six years to my mother, as I'm now the main carer for my mother-in-law, aged eighty-four, who still lives with us. She is still a daunting character who is demanding and set in her ways but I wouldn't have it any other way.

My aspiration is now to create in myself a 'new style of mother-in-law' where I can support my daughters-in-law to achieve their own ambitions in their careers whatever they may be; to allow them the freedom and space within our extended household to bring up their children the way they want. To have four generations under one roof is complex and emotionally draining at times; however, I hope the benefits and support surrounding us all will help us be patient and remember how blessed we are.

I just wish my parents were alive today to witness their great-grandchildren flourish and me receive my OBE from the Queen so as to prove that hard work is recognised, not just in spite of, but often thanks to our background and upbringing.

Kamel receiving her OBE from Her Majesty The Queen

Then and now: Kamel and her family

THREE

The Show Must Go On
SARITA SABHARWAL

I was the most excited person that day when I received her reply on Facebook Messenger. Usually I listen to her on the drive-time show when driving back from work. But this time, I wanted to exclusively hear her story – where she began and how she made it here. As I made myself comfortable and set up my camera to begin our interview, she looked at our information pack and said, "Listen, I must tell you something before we begin. I have not had to struggle in life to make it this far. Somehow, things have just fallen into my lap. I don't think I'm the right person to talk to." I looked at her and smiled. "Yes, you are," I said, "I need you to show the world that destiny can be generous too, at times." And this was my most gratifying interview to date.

AASTHA K SINGHANIA

I always wanted to become a singer so I could lend my voice to the microphones for India to hear. Now, many people in the United Kingdom hear me five times a week on their radio. My dreams came true but not in the way I had planned. Instead of singing harmonious tunes, my profession became presenting; selecting trending tunes for others to listen to. My name is Sarita Sabharwal and I am a radio presenter. This is my story.

I was born on 29 September 1954 in New Delhi, India, amongst four sisters and a brother. Being the youngest, I was very pampered in the company of my older sisters. I completed my bachelor's degree in Arts from Kamala Nehru University, New Delhi, and also did my '*Sangeet Visharad*' simultaneously from Prayag University, Allahabad, India. Although I was never a brilliant student all through my education, I managed to complete my singing training with a Distinction.

My passion for singing, which was so evidently visible from a young age, caught a lot of people's attention in Allahabad, who duly guided me to All India Radio. Their guidance got me started off as a freelance singer on a youth forum called '*YuvAvani*', where I was scheduled to sing for fifteen minutes, every six weeks. I did a couple of similar shows before I hosted my first radio talk show called '*Mehfil*', at the age of sixteen. From then to now, I have not had to look back or pause to breathe. It wasn't needed and neither did I want to slow down. Even when I moved to the UK after marriage in 1975, I found work straight away – although not in radio initially. Still, life was always fast paced.

'Kismet' plays a very important role in our lives. Destiny and fate coupled with hard work is the best recipe to reach your aim. In my case, I can proudly say I never had to struggle, never had to ask for work. I thank the Almighty for letting opportunities fall into my lap. Not many people get this and I feel blessed to be in such a place. Since the age of sixteen, I have been on the go, managing multiple work projects in different places. After marriage, things did not change. I immediately started looking for jobs and found myself working for Wall's Meat Company in the accounts department. After serving the company for ten years, I was offered redundancy as they moved further north in England. As a result of my redundancy, in that period I settled down in this new country, had three children and had a life with my family, which I was happy in.

But, as they say, once you've worked for it, you will always yearn for it. My heart still belonged to the radio industry. At that time, there used to be one single show on LBC Radio and I personally didn't think much of the presenter. I knew I could do a better job. Curiously, I called up the BBC and spoke to them about how I could get involved as a singer on their radio channel. They directed me to their only (multi-cultural?) show, *Naya Zindagi Naya Jeevan*, which at the time was run from Birmingham. I wrote to Mr Mahendra Kaul, who was their main presenter, asking for a chance to work on the show. However, I did not receive any response. To this day, I think of what would have happened if he had actually replied and let me sing. Life would have been different for me and I, probably, would not have deflected towards presenting. But like I always believe, no one can take your fate from you. I was always meant to be where I am today after crossing all the hurdles that came my way.

My introduction to presenting happened in 1986 when I happened to meet Dr Avtar Lit, who was heading Sina Radio at the time. He auditioned me and I started working for them immediately. I worked voluntarily and did a few recorded shows. But this didn't last long and I quit because it didn't seem to be a very viable option financially. I felt balanced and more in control of my family and work whilst working at the London Borough of Ealing Council, which was my full-time job at the time. It was only in 1989, when Dr Lit acquired a radio licence, that my journey at Sunrise Radio began.

By 1991, I had become a popular voice and the audience favoured my shows. Opportunities started knocking at my door and one fine day, I was approached for TV. I went to meet the directors of TV Asia, Javed Pasha (also known as JP) and Faisal, and while having an informal chat they suddenly asked me to drop my job at Ealing Council and to start working for them – starting the very next day. They were even ready to pay me for the notice period I was to serve at the council. Quite taken aback, I asked for some time, so I could discuss it with my family, but they wouldn't let me leave until I gave them an answer. They made me call my husband straight away, but he handed the decision back to me. The next day I wrote my resignation letter and submitted it at the council, re-directing my route to become a presenter at TV Asia.

Politics and me are like a set of parallel lines and I believed there was no chance of me ever becoming a news presenter. But rather amusingly in hindsight, on my first day at TV Asia I was told to present the News. Unwillingly, and with a lot of resistance, I pushed myself with this title for a month or two. As if this was not enough, JP one day came to me and insisted that I leave Sunrise Radio due to conflicted interests. Radio was my passion and it was only with continuous persistence from JP that I had to give in.

Dr Lit was upset with my decision and I had a heavy heart too. I left my job at Sunrise without prior notice, right in the middle of my show, which was quite unprofessional on my part. However, that evening, JP came to my house and took me to an unknown building near Brent Cross. On entering I realised it was the broadcasting house for Spectrum Radio, a channel which TV Asia used, hiring eight hours of airtime and naming it Radio Asia. My co-presenter, Asif Ghazali, and myself took on the role of managing and broadcasting from Spectrum, something JP knew I could handle beautifully. For three years, my schedule remained very frenzied. My day started with my breakfast show from 6am to 8am at Spectrum. I used to come home, get the children ready and leave for my job at TV Asia, which would finish at 6pm. I would go home, feed the children and step out one more time to do my second radio show from 7.30pm to 9pm.

My hard work started to show when in three consecutive years I received the Best Radio Show and Best Presenter awards. Through my show, I interviewed luminaries from all walks of life. From doctors to film stars, from politicians to musicians, I have had the honour to sit with so many people from India and the UK. For me to work so hard required a strong backbone, provided by my husband and children. I could not have come this far if it wasn't for them. Every morning when I came back from my morning radio show, my husband would get the children ready for school. My children, too, never complained and continued to grow beautifully all those years.

In roughly 1994, Zee TV took over TV Asia and downsized massively. Under JP, I had the opportunity to contribute so much to the channel but Zee TV reduced my shows to one show a week. This resulted in a mental and financial setback and I, personally, consider that period as a rough one. For TV Asia, I had made a big career move by leaving my job at Ealing Council and Sunrise – one that had helped me financially and the other which had enhanced my talent. Zee TV had also pulled out of Spectrum Radio and that had left a big void in my life.

From my show on TV Asia, I was in touch with an astrologer, Ms Bhavna Pota, who called me one day to ask if I was interested in working with Namastey TV. Desperate that I was, I took on that offer immediately and started working for them. During the shoot for a commercial advertisement at Himalayan Carpets, I met with Mr Deepak Vishwanath, the owner of Asianet TV. He had heard of me and offered me a role on his channel. I happily made the switch. I started with one show a week and by the time I left the company, I was hosting seven shows every week. It was during my time at Asianet that I once hosted a charity show where Channi Singh, lead singer of the group Alaap, was invited to be a judge. In conversation with him, he asked why I wouldn't return to Sunrise. I told him my apprehensions and how scared and guilty I felt to have let Dr Lit down by choosing TV Asia over him. The next day, Mr Singh arranged a meeting with Dr Lit for me. I look back on that day as nothing less than a miracle. Dr Lit happily took me back to the radio station in 1995 and within two days I was back on air with my voice. I hosted my show from 10am to 12pm and went on to continue my day job with Asianet. Asianet went into liquidation in 2000 and I continued to be with Sunrise till 2014. In 2014, Sunrise went into liquidation and was taken over by Lyca. I was asked to continue working with them and joined as Programming Manager. Today I host my drive-time show from 5pm to 7pm at Lyca Dil Se on 1035 AM. About thirty-five freelance presenters work under me and I manage a variety of shows that go on air.

All through my life, I have never sat at home thinking where to go for work or who would employ me next. There was never a plan that I consciously made. Life takes you where you need to go and nothing can change its course or destination. Even between jobs, I did a whole lot of freelance work, from hosting different events to recording the introductory message for Virgin Atlantic. Lots of museum tours used to play Hindi translation voiceovers recorded by me. I feel humbled and ecstatic sitting right now and going back in time, which brought me close to so many dignitaries. My interview with Benazir Bhutto, for almost seventy-five minutes, remains etched in my memory. I have also had the honour to share the stage with Lady Diana at a council event in East London.

My journey, as I mentioned before, has not been one of struggles. Yes, I have had hurdles, which I approached and addressed with dignity and grace. Like most professionals, I too went through politics at work but I have never wished ill upon anyone. People were jealous, people were curious; some also tried to sabotage my presence on television in their own way. But I did not let any of this affect my karma, the fruits of which I receive now. To be in this industry and to have stayed on firmly for so many years is tough. It is even tougher to hold many years to your credit without losing one's dignity and grace. Work came to me in a flow and one thing led to another. I wouldn't have been able to do all this without my support system. My husband was my biggest support and together we have come a long way. Today we feel blessed to see our children well settled with beautiful partners and even special grandchildren. Times are different now and there is so much talent out there for us to explore. The world of radio and television will always be spreading, strengthening and soaring high. We all seem to be running a race to slow down eventually. Take a moment and breathe. It is only when you stop and look around that you will know who is with you and who you have left behind. It is then that you can analyse how many people you may have hurt in the process and how many injured you. The only thing I have lived by is this:

Kabhi bhool ke bhi na karo,
Kissi se salook aisa,
Jo koi tumse kare,
Toh na gavara ho.
(Do to others as you would have them do to you)

Sarita with music director Naushad Ali (second left)

Sarita with Shahrukh Khan

Sarita with Sushmita Sen

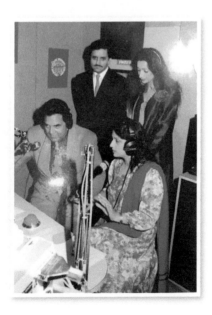

Sarita with Dharmendra

FOUR

A SAVVI Life

RITA CHOWDHRY

Rita runs her own coaching and consultancy company for businesses and individuals who feel they want to fulfil their potential in their professional or personal lives. Prior to this, she ran her own property business for twenty-five years alongside teaching Business and Economics at secondary level and progressing to university level. Her experience as a qualified behaviour consultant and experienced coach provide a real insight into human behaviour. When Rita shared her story with me over the two days that we were together, we cried, laughed and reflected on her journey. Her story is beautifully told with an open heart.

ANITA GOYAL

He died in the street, my father, surrounded by people too busy helping themselves to his forfeited belongings to heed his last breath. The driver survived, the passenger on the other side survived. My father was on his way from the airport to his home town in Ludhiana to visit his parents – it was the summer holidays. He'd taken a taxi with some other passengers he'd met on the plane and his taxi had a head-on collision with a truck. I was only nine, but I remember it well – the sound of my aunty knocking frantically against the wooden door. "Your husband has died in a car crash." There was so much screaming after that.

Death, to me, had always been this far away thing, a sad scene in someone else's life. My only experience with it had been those announcements on the news and radio, broadcasting the names of victims in the latest IRA bombing.

I don't think I cried that night. It just hadn't registered yet, despite the house being full of people and their eyes brimming with pity. It hit me in the morning – that awful hollow feeling as my mum packed her bags and flew to India, with my brother in tow.

That feeling stuck around the entire two weeks she was gone. It stayed with me, as my sister and other brother were handed back and forth between one set of family friends and the next. My mother had gone to India for the funeral, but she didn't quite make it in time. It was August; the depth of summer meant they couldn't keep the body, so they had laid her husband to rest without her.

It was two straight weeks of waking up in strangers' homes, missing my mum and just wanting her back. But when she came back, she was someone else. She'd fallen off a rickshaw and lost a tooth. She had also lost weight, and what was left of her was wrapped in a white sari that was never meant for the bracing cold of Wolverhampton in winter. No makeup, no jewellery; she stayed that way for years. That was the first time I remember thinking how cruel the Indian community could be.

When we lost my dad, we had to live by values that were the common denominator of the Asian community. My mum felt that these were the people she would now have to rely upon. *They're going to help support me now, they'll make judgements on me, they will be the people that will introduce my kids to potential partners.* So, she took us by the hand and led us into this overarching shadow. Now, I can look back on it and think of the values we inherited from our Asian culture, and how they got us through that stage in our lives. There was that sense of community spirit, the way people came and supported us. But there were so many judgements that simply felt unnecessarily harsh. Now that I work with clients, I make them examine which of their values and beliefs are serving them to be happy and fulfilled and consciously create and live by values and beliefs and discard those that are not.

My dad, when he was alive, was an incredibly intelligent man. As a younger gentleman, he had studied History, but in the years before his death, his bookshelf had become laden with personal development books. He had taken us out of the inner city, to the suburbs. A three-bedroom, semi-detached house with all the trimmings: indoor bathroom, front garden, back garden, driveway… All of this in a community where the people that looked like us were bus drivers and steel factory workers.

My mother had been a housewife in a foreign country with four young children. Now, overnight, she had to take on the responsibility of the household income. She had been fully educated, and trained as a teacher in India. But to qualify by English standards, she would have had to complete a conversion course and wherever was she to find the time for that? Thankfully, my father had developed a property portfolio. The job at hand was to go to the property, sign the rent book and collect the rent. My mother couldn't drive. It would take her seven tries to qualify for her licence but, in the meantime, a good friend of my father helped her, going with her to collect the rent and such. Still, every night for the first year, we could hear her crying herself to sleep because she just couldn't see how she was going to make ends meet.

We all had to pull together to survive. Whatever help we could give my mum, we offered. For instance, the job of cleaning the house belonged to myself and my sister. We'd wake on a Saturday morning, clean the house and then catch the bus into town to do the food shopping for Mum, so she could get on with other things. What's interesting is that we never questioned it. We saw how hard she was working and I guess we just sort of fell in line. Hard work and resilience were values we – my siblings and I – learnt from our mum and they have carried us to where and who we are now. But looking back, there were a few values and beliefs that I wished she had challenged.

I didn't go away to university because my mum needed me at home. It was the same old story, what would people think? We had a similar conversation about jobs, i.e. you can't get a job because I don't want people to think that I'm so hard up for money that I have to send my daughters out to work. Even as I say this, however, I don't want to give the impression that she suppressed or imprisoned me. She gave me the space and freedom to do as I pleased (within reason) but at the same time, instilled a voice into the back of my head that would habitually ask, *Well, what will people think?* The community expected us to conform to certain stereotypes and my mother accepted them as she depended on the community. Had my father been alive, he would have challenged them.

I carried that with me, whether I meant to or not, throughout my life. When I had a miscarriage, when my son was diagnosed with vitiligo at five and then dyslexia at six, it was that voice that came to me before anything else: *What will people think? Will they think I lost the baby because I was too careless? What will they think if my son doesn't get good grades?* That was my default, my conditioning at work. But eventually, I came to realise that nothing I did would ever stop them from talking about me or my family. If I appeased the community on one matter, they'd simply find something else to criticise. I could almost handle it when it came to myself. I could deal with their archaic notions of what a woman was supposed to be, but when their judgements began to impact my children, I had to draw the line.

I had trained as a teacher, following in the footsteps of both my mother and my father. And my passion has always been to help others learn and develop so to teach was an obvious choice.

When confronted with the problem of my son's dyslexia, I drew from my mother's strength, trying to remember that this was nothing compared to what she went through. I remember how often she'd remark – in regard to all the things she juggled – "Oh, I just do it because I have to, for my kids' sake." Now it was my turn. As a teacher, I knew how large a role mindset played in success, and I decided that I wouldn't let my son be counted out. So, I left work and did a postgraduate diploma in teaching children with specific learning difficulties. I decided that it didn't matter if teachers gave up on him because I never would.

The most important thing I think I learnt from pursuing that diploma was the devastating impact that learning difficulties can have on a child's self-confidence. I had to focus him on his strengths, keep him confident and self-assured. Sure enough, he got into those good private schools, with offers from top universities, and the rest is history. But without my mother, without those values of perseverance and a strong family ethic that she passed on to me, which I, in turn, handed down to my own children, I'm not sure how this story would have ended.

With that said, I cannot overstress the importance of the time I spent in reflection, which allowed me to examine the values that had been passed on to me, and challenge the ones that failed to serve my happiness. For instance, I inherited from my mother a tendency to worry. Once my father passed, she began to habitually worry about the future. Both she and – to a larger extent – our circumstances had an impact on my once optimistic mindset and I too began to worry that the worst would happen. When I met my husband, Jeff, I used to think simultaneously of how nice a guy he was and how much I would hate to lose him. I used to think about him getting sick, or him dying the way my father did. When there were highs, I'd never let myself enjoy them because I was too busy worrying, following in my mum's footsteps. I sheepishly admit that it was indeed my husband who liberated me. He was a different breed to everyone else I'd ever met. He was very much about speaking your mind, doing what you want, following your ambitions and having a healthy mindset, and frankly it was a breath of fresh air!

Jeff was the first person I had been introduced to in London. I was immediately blown away by him. He was unwaveringly intelligent; he read the *Financial Times*, had been to university and now worked in the City. We hit it off right away. That said, both our families were in somewhat of a rush for us to get married. My sister had got engaged before me, but my mum wouldn't let her get married because it wasn't right for one's youngest daughter to be wed until the eldest had first been paired off.

To an Indian woman, there is only one label to be concerned with: that of a good wife. My husband never saw it that way; he wanted – sometimes more than I did – for me to have the freedom to be myself. You want to go back to work, go back to work. You don't want to work, don't work. Run the house, buy some properties, do whatever you want.

It was a type of freedom I'd never known, but I stress that word: type. My childhood was never that of a caged bird, but there were certain things I knew the community had deemed unfit for a girl and I never wanted anyone to point a finger at my mother and say you were a bad mother; that would break her heart.

Even in the rebellion of my teenage years, I would never have been seen walking around Wolverhampton in the company of men or boys. My mum wouldn't have minded *per se*, but it was something I simply wouldn't consider doing in case it reflected badly on her.

Thinking back, I see now that the circumstances forced me and my siblings to become adults overnight. In one way or another, we all took on some of the burden of filling the hole left in our lives by my father's passing. For instance, I knew my dad loved teaching and education, so I became their guardian. "You've got to do your homework," said the twelve-year-old to the four-year-old. It's funny now, but at the time it seemed like the most important thing in the world. My mum used to say, "Rita, you should've been the boy and your brother should've been the girl." What she was referring to, I later came to learn, was my dominant drive and ambitious character, which is associated with male characteristics.

After I got married, we moved from Hounslow and I decided that I wanted a house. Not just any house. It had to be a big house, in a green, leafy area. A house that I had always dreamed of. I always loved interior design and from a young age I had a picture in my mind of the home I would like; I made that into reality. It was a three-bedroom house which we converted to a five-bedroom, each with its own en suite. Nobody in our social circle had even one en suite; why do you need five? Why do you need three reception rooms? They didn't get it, but these were my dreams. What else was I to do but chase them?

Unfortunately, the unsolicited critiques kept coming. When we sent our kids to private school, it was, why are the state schools not good enough? When we hired some help, it became, don't you think it's too indulgent to have a cleaner when your wife is working part-time? But now I was beginning to live a life that was not limited by others, Jeff and I designed our life to be the best and happiest it could be.

I had to learn to justify myself, even if only to myself. When I went back to work, I reasoned that, if I could make sure that my kids were well looked after, there was no inherent issue. If I could pay for childcare that was equal to, or better than, that which I could provide, then no one was losing out emotionally, or financially.

For me, the main purpose of working was never for money. It was about my own, personal, emotional growth. I think we all tend to look at our role in a relationship and try and calculate our own worth, but there are some things that simply can't be prescribed to numbers. If you were to put a formula to it, it's actually worth a woman going to work, because the inherent costs of childcare and housekeeping will overshadow her financial contributions. With that said, however, to deny a woman the right to work would be to take our entire society back some 200 years. If I didn't work, I wouldn't be the best person I could be, as my passion and motivator is to grow and develop myself and others. That fire inside my belly made me a better mother and wife, but more importantly, it made me a better me.

Then one day, I woke up and realised that I'd got to the stage in my life where my children were independent and, simply put, didn't need me. When they were younger, I'd been dedicated to supporting their growth and development and since I was a teacher, my passion was being met and my strengths were being used. But now two of my children had degrees mounted on the wall, I fell into something between a comfort zone and a rut. I still had so much potential and a desire for growth and fulfilment to take myself to another level.

I had left teaching, I was doing a lot of reading and somewhere in there it was my brother who decided that what I needed was psychic intervention. When this supposed psychic asked who I wanted to connect with, my first and only answer was my father.

Deep down, I think I wanted to hear those words: *Well done, Rita.* I think I was hoping that he'd be proud that I'd become a teacher, that I was the only one of my siblings to get my degree. That's not quite what I got, however.

He described my father perfectly. It was as though his character was sitting right there – his stack of books, the pens in his pocket and a few other facts about him that made me sit up and pay attention. Then he said, "Rita, your father is asking why you haven't pushed yourself more." When I asked why, he replied, "You've got so much more to give. You've just limited yourself." That was the catalyst I needed.

I was shocked and a little disappointed but, in truth, that was exactly what my father would have said. He would have told me that I could do so much more with my life and, as usual, he would have been right. But please do not take this as an admission of remorse. Not for a second do I regret the way I spent my life. My three children are phenomenal people and I wouldn't trade the time I've spent with them for anything in the world. But that reading was exactly the kick I needed, at exactly the right time. So, I decided I was going to start my own business, and just like that I started my transformation.

I went back and read my father's favourite book. It was called *How to Win Friends and Influence People.* After that, someone recommended another, called *The Monk Who Sold His Ferrari.* It was about looking at your life and finding your passion and, indeed, your purpose. I remember thinking, *Perhaps I should get a coach and figure out what I want to do.* And then that turned into, *You know, I think I want to be a coach.*

Life is funny sometimes, even in its cruelty. Soon after I started training, we lost Jeff's mum to cancer. It was just weeks after her diagnosis; she lay in her son's arms and took her final breath. Three months later, I lost my mum, too. She was there when my mother-in-law died. She went into a bit of a depression and her weakened immune system left her prey to a series of infections. She ended up in hospital and, eventually, she passed. I'm not quite sure what happened after that or where I got the strength from but I became a different person.

My mum always said to me, "Rita, I know out of all of my kids, when I pass away, you're the one that's not going to be able to cope." Ever since my dad's passing, I would cry at the drop of a hat. Anything happy, anything sad. My nieces and nephews used to say, "Aunty, you're the only one that will cry when there's a supermarket opening." But that's the thing about happiness, it makes you miss the people who taught you what it was. The day of my wedding, I couldn't enjoy it because all I kept thinking about was, *My dad should be here.*

My son Reece, my firstborn – what makes me so proud of him is his determination, hard work and above all how spiritual he is. From a young age he has lived strongly by the principle of karma. In his teens, a group of his friends were just messing around in the local neighbourhood and decided to play tricks on an elderly couple by repeatedly frightening them by knocking at the front door and running and throwing eggs at their house. Reece did the difficult thing of walking away from his friends and refusing to take part. His friends became abusive to him with the intention of trying to make him take part but he stayed true to his values and didn't succumb to peer pressure. The elderly couple identified one of the boys as a local and reported them to the police; it resulted in the boys being questioned at the local police station and receiving a warning. The other parents of the boys personally congratulated Reece for having the guts to walk away and stick to his principles and values. He now runs his own venture capital business; he will only invest in businesses that have strong values that are compatible to his.

My daughter Leah is a compassionate philanthropist. Her first visit to India at the age of seven left her so disturbed by the poverty she observed that she committed to making a difference through taking on personal challenges. She gave up sweets and fizzy drinks at the age of seven to raise money for children who were blind in India. She raised £11,000 running the London Marathon for LILY Against Human Trafficking. Her greatest achievement is being the first British Asian woman to swim the English Channel, in an incredible fourteen hours and forty-four minutes, raising a phenomenal £105,000 for Cancer Research UK and £45,000 for the British Asian Trust. What is unique about Leah's fundraising is that each time she puts herself through physical and mental challenges to help others. This was an incredible ordeal, both physically and emotionally, where she scarified her social life by training up to twenty hours a week in the last few months leading up to the swim.

A total commitment of eighteen months' training and 1.5 stone of weight gain is extremely demanding. This is incredible for someone of her personality who likes to stay in her comfort zone. During her six-hour qualifier she nearly gave up; swimming in the dark, cold water at around fourteen degrees, against overpowering waves, she felt like she was going to die. She felt she had underestimated the ordeal. When she called me from Croatia, we discussed how she was physically capable but she had allowed her mind to become fearful. I used some of the SAVVI framework techniques that I have created and use with my clients on controlling her mind to help her get through this. Within days she changed her mindset and successfully completed the six-hour trial. She is driven by her desire to help others that are helpless.

Anya, my youngest daughter – I admire how fearless she is and lives life to the full. From a young age she has appeared on stage singing and acting, playing a small part in a film directed by Madonna! Anya courageously questioned Boris Johnson on Sky News about his ambitions to be Prime Minister; Boris was left lost for words as he struggled to hide his true emotions. Anya is constantly breaking down stereotypes of what Asian girls should do and say. She puts herself out of her comfort zone and does things that even grown adults fear. My youngest is not afraid to speak out for causes and that's why she is passionate about going into politics.

The day I watched the life drain from my mother's eyes was the day I truly found courage, for what is left to be afraid of after that? But I don't say that in bitterness, or with spite in my heart for that which is inevitable. For after that day, my life found its natural light, and I found strength I didn't know I had.

It was time to take risks, face up to some challenges. I wanted to start a business, so what were the costs involved? Well, I was fortunate enough to be in a place of comfort so if I set up a business and it didn't succeed… so what?

I set up my business, SAVRAN. I named it after my mum and my mother-in-law: Savitri and Rani. My mother and mother-in-law's legacy continue to inspire the work that I do. I fill up with pride when I hear someone else call out "SAVRAN" (say at an awards' night or when I hear my Head of Client Services call up a client to make arrangements for a workshop for their board of directors). Hearing my mother's and my mother-in-law's names being used daily means that their legacy lives on beyond their lives; I feel they're both still here with me. I hope that I'm making them proud of the work I continue to do in their name – particularly when I receive industry recognition for my work (Best Newcomer of the Year – International Coaching Awards 2015; Best Small Business Coach – International Business Awards 2016; Best Coach – Best Business Women Awards 2016; Service Award Finalist 2017 – Toast of Surrey Business Awards).

It was my mother who instilled in me the value of giving back and helping others. I'm passionate about upholding that value using all my strengths. That value has led me to search for new causes to support outside my coaching. So, I'm a school governor for a short-stay school for pupils who've been expelled from mainstream education. I also provide *pro bono* leadership coaching (through the Uprising Programme) for young adults from minority ethnic groups. I am in the process of setting up a mentoring system for children in India, and look forward to offering *pro bono* services to school teachers in India. All these projects inspire me as a coach with their respective challenges.

I will leave you with this message:

Always know your strengths to overcome any of your weaknesses. Discover your passion and use it! Challenge those values and beliefs that are not serving you, create strong values and beliefs that will help you be your happiest and most fulfilled. Most of all give back to others; this is the most fulfilling thing in life. These are the principles of SAVVI that I now share with my clients and I feel blessed that I have the opportunity to help others lead a more fulfilled and happier personal and professional life.

Rita with her family (top from left: Rita, Anya, Leah, Jeff;
front: bride Anila and groom Reece)

Rita with her mother

Rita's father

FIVE

Iron Lady
RAJ NAYYAR

How do you picture a ninety-year-old in your mind? You'd be forgiven for picturing an ailing, weak, frail person, with people around to make sure she is looked after.

I was not ready to believe that Raj was turning ninety this year. I got to know about her through a very close friend of hers, when I was speaking about this project. She seemed to match all the criteria I needed in a woman for this book. Upon coming face to face with her, I realised, in the truest sense, that age is just a number. It's all in the mind and you can be as weak or strong as you want yourself to be. Her zest for life has not disappeared; her knowledge about the world hasn't diminished. Still very aware, she remembered all the dates and years in narrating this story to me. For me, she is an iron lady – fearless, incorrigible, valiant and so much more progressive than you and I together could ever be.

AASTHA K SINGHANIA

It seems like there is still something I need to do. Since my childhood, I have set goals that seemed right for my family and myself, making sure no obstacle or difficulty prevented me from reaching them. Today, I sit here with no regrets, knowing that I have spent almost ninety years of my life acting with this same belief. I have been a fighter ever since I was young, and had to learn from an early age to stand on my own two feet. I was born at a time when not many were allowed to voice their thoughts, especially women. My father, like in most families, had established control over his people – a family of fifteen (thirteen children, my mother and himself). He was a doctor and he lived with authority; no one could think of uttering a word against his thoughts. There were times when he would raise his hand at my mother and there I would stand, with my hands on my waist and question her: "Why won't you leave him? Look at the way he treats you." But my mother would shut me up, flabbergasted at what I had said to her.

My mother never liked me, for she thought I was too forward in my thinking. If I had to compare my childhood to anything, I would draw a parallel to *Malgudi Days*[1]. All of us were naughty to the extent that we were famously known as 'Syal Sisters'. We were beaten up by our teachers, fought and scratched our friends and sisters, and often schemed and planned to embarrass our 'target of the day'. We would not take any nonsense from anyone. A very famous anecdote from my time in college in Lahore got me known as a 'lioness'. I was given a bicycle to use for my commute to college, which had no brakes. My mother felt that I wouldn't need anything more than two wheels attached to a rod, which could take

---

1   A collection of short stories, written by R.K. Narayan.

me from one place to another. I could not even get on or off myself and somebody had to come to my rescue every time. One time, I crashed into a couple walking on the road and the word spread throughout the college campus. One of the boys tried to tease me and my instant reaction was to take my sandal off so I could beat him up. My professor, upon hearing this, took me to our girls' common room and, instead of punishing me, exemplified me by saying, "Be like her and do not tolerate any unacceptable behaviour."

On the other hand, my father adored me. He knew I would become something someday, and he hoped to see me become a doctor like him. I think I wanted that too. My father retired in 1940 and we moved to Lahore – a time from which I have beautiful memories. We stayed in close proximity with Muslims, who were great friends of our family. Huge gardens surrounded our house and, every evening, all the children would assemble in our gardens to play to their heart's content. Within a few years the word 'partition' came to be spoken about and I wanted to help in any way I could. In the evening, boys and girls of my college used to come together and hold meetings. My mother refused to let me step out of the house but my father thought I was brave enough to handle this and allowed me to attend the gatherings. Even the Superintendent of Police, who was a childhood friend of my father's, warned him to control me or else I would land in jail like the other protestors. But I was stubborn and was adamant to be of any service I could to my country.

I was an ardent admirer of Mahatma Gandhi (Bapu) and followed his idealist principles. At the time, Gandhi was in his ashram in Khulna, Bangladesh, and I was insistent on meeting him. Immediately taking a train to West Bengal, I tried to persuade my sister-in-law to come with me to

Khulna, but she was scared and tried hard to keep me from going all the way to meet him. I did not budge and eventually she came around; our quest to find Bapu had begun. We searched for him for a few days and were just about ready to give up hope. With one last try, I climbed the wall of the ashram and peered closely to get a good look of the place. I lost my grip and fell straight into the garden, right at Bapu's feet where he was taking his evening walk with his nieces. He looked at me as if I had fallen from the skies. I asked if he would let me go to the villages and help him serve the country but he wasn't happy with the idea and said, "You look very young to be going by yourself. We would have to send at least two men for your protection. Why don't you come back when you're twenty-one, with all your dowry that has been saved for you if you're not married." I said, "Bapu, there is a lot of time before that day will come, can I please help you in some way?" After a lot of thought Bapu asked me to meet his two representatives at the Congress headquarters in Lahore and correspond with his nieces, who actively guided me with the freedom movement from that side of the country.

My father was never happy about my enthusiasm and participation in the Indian independence movement. The moment I turned sixteen, everyone wanted me to tie the knot with the first person they came across. Fortunately, due to my strong-headedness, I did not give in to their wishes. I was desperate to work and lead my country to independence. If not, I had made up my mind to study abroad. My father introduced me to a man from the United Kingdom and eventually I agreed, spending sixty-five years of marriage with him. We had a simple wedding on 15 October 1946, with a whole lot of conditions stated by me, including no dowry, no unnecessary religious customs, no jewellery and no *band baja baraat*[2]. Bhag, my husband, agreed to all of this and within a month I came to London.

Before coming to London, I visited my in-laws' house in Phillaur, Punjab. My sister-in-law was amazed at my values and seemed surprised at the way I handled my responsibilities in their house. I could cook, whatever little was taught to me. I wouldn't listen to anything wrong about my husband's family even when provoked by her, and I knew how to show respect in ways expected of me. Somehow, my mother-in-law was quite modern, and I requested her not to impose *ghoongat*[3] on us daughters-in-law. I asked her, "Why would only the daughters-in-law be expected to be in a veil and not the daughters? Am I not like your daughter?" She couldn't refuse and happily agreed as long as I did not say or do anything wrong.

London, in November, was dull, rainy, cold and miserable. No one was there to welcome us and I wasn't sure how I would cope with this. I was already pregnant and had to settle myself in these conditions. I did not have basic shoes or clothes equipped for the weather and neither was there food that I was used to. No chapatti, no rice; my husband used to go to the London dockside to bring a pound of rice from Indian sailors or Punjabi '*vadi*' from the Indian restaurant. I came with a few silk sarees, a couple of Punjabi suits and two pairs of trousers. Bhag and I used to go house hunting in the deep snow, with me wearing my silk

2   A customary wedding procession from the groom and his family, travelling to the wedding venue to bring the bride back with him.

3   Purdah system, covering the daughter-in-law's face by a veil.

saree and slippers. In April, I found a four-bedroom house that we liked and we moved in before the baby arrived.

During this time, Bhag and his younger brother were working in partnership with his uncle in the garment business that was started by the uncle's family. However, his wife was never happy to see the profits being shared amongst the three. When we moved to London, we stayed in their house for six months and there was not a single day when she did not let me feel her misery in some way or another. The day we moved out of that house, the uncle withdrew all the money from the account and we moved without a single penny. It is only through the kindness of God that we never felt any financial pressure, as my husband continued the business with his brother in equal partnership, independent of his uncle.

I went back to India in 1948. A lot had changed since I had moved to London; I had a baby girl in my arms, and my family had moved to Nainital, India. The time during Partition was a nightmare for me; there was no contact and we had no idea where they all were. It was only later that we found out they were all safe and I could not wait to see them. My brother-in-law accompanied me and stayed with me wherever I went. In Nainital, he confessed his desire to marry my younger sister, Pushpa. Luckily my sister was thrilled with the idea of being in London with me and happily agreed to the nuptial. My father, however, was completely against the proposal and believed that I had coaxed her into marrying Bhag's brother. He felt that marrying two daughters away to a foreign land would mean seeing less of us, which was true to an extent. But he gave in after I assured him how happy I was and what a wonderful life my sister would have with us around her.

After my brother-in-law got married to Pushpa, my husband told me that they could afford to send only one of us at a time to visit our parents. I respected his judgement and understood that we were a joint family with one pot of income. But I was desperate to visit India and my family, and started thinking of ways to earn some money of my own so I could have an independent spending hand. In those days, my niece and her husband were in London for career training and were actively looking for a house. The *Evening Standard* would advertise for a flat almost every day, but if by the evening they went to look at it, it was said to be 'occupied'. This happened once, twice, again and again. Racial discrimination was very prevalent at that time and I decided to raise my voice against it. I had saved some of the money that my father had given me. My husband helped me get a mortgage and I bought my first flat in Cricklewood, London. In response to what my niece had gone through, I advertised for 'Blacks and Browns only'. However, within three years I had to bite my tongue because none of them knew how to keep the place intact.

It was during this time I realised what having your own money meant. I felt independent and was not obliged to ask for money to go to India anymore. I started developing properties, buying and reselling, and at one time had seventeen flats in London. My business grew and kept me busy – a venture from which I retired only three years ago. I firmly believe that looking after a house, family and children is a duty for both parents to take on. As a wife and lady of the house, I took care of all the finances and investments. As a daughter-in-law, I made sure I lived up to all the expectations that were meted out to me. As a mother, I left no stone unturned to give my children the best of what they deserved. Unfortunately, the vision I had for my children was never fulfilled. My children never received the happiness that I got from life and my husband. My daughter, Geeta, and I always had a conflict of interest whether about her education, her ambition, or her marriage. Love failed her and at one point she almost gave up on life. Today, she suffers from bipolar disorder but she channels all her grief and suffering by making sculptures, something she does so beautifully. My son, Anil, has been my pillar and shoulder. Love failed him too but he mustered himself and today is a grandfather of two lovely children.

Life has been a miracle. In 1972, I was diagnosed with ovarian cancer and had to undergo chemotherapy, which made me very weak. It took me six years to recover but in 1978 I found that my tumour had returned. My bones had become so brittle that I suffered four fractures within those years. I was scared to go through the pain I went through last time but the researcher begged and made me believe in this new treatment that they had discovered. I was operated upon and medicines were given, which made me have convulsions; my state didn't seem to be any better. The chemo also induced painful side effects; osteoporosis had set in, with me losing 3.5 inches in height. I had thirteen fractures with a broken spine. But after all that, my tumour never came back, a complete eradication.

The Women India Association began in the UK in 1961 with the vision and foresightedness of Her Excellency Mrs Vijaya Lakshmi Pandit. I joined the association in 1962 when I felt I could be of help in taking this noble cause forward. During my illness in 1972, I had to take a break from working with the charity but after my cancer, I came back and donated my thirty-six-carat diamond engagement ring to the Cancer Research Society at our gala ball. With every ball, we have been fortunate to multiply the amount of money donated. But all of this is just a drop in the ocean. There is so much more we need to give back to humanity, to women and to those who need it the most. It has been fifty-six years, and I still feel very strongly about it. I am so proud to see that the younger generation have stepped up and are now taking the reins in making this world a better place for women across the globe.

If I were in India, life would not have been the same. I may have not married so early, or may not have got the opportunity to become so financially independent. But I still would have said 'no' to dowry, 'no' to oppression and 'no' to ageing. I am ninety, and I still have dreams to fulfil. This autumn, I am set to see the Grand Canyon, gamble a little as I love casinos, and experience whatever is left of my life with a smile on my face. My children are devoted to me and I have a lovely family around me. But to all of you who are reading this, the only thing I ask is to please speak your mind, say what gives you happiness and do not wait for a lifetime to do what you always planned to. You must understand that 'no' is a word which can be used without guilt. Every woman has to fight, even now, for things that are our rights. We need to change the air, the attitude that refuses to change. Help yourself and you will help all evolve.

Raj with her husband, Bhag

Raj with her sister, Pushpa

Six

Daughter of Amritsar
BARONESS SANDIP VERMA

Baroness Sandip Verma is an Indian-English politician and, as a member of the House of Lords, was the Parliamentary Under-Secretary of State for International Development from May 2015 to July 2016. She is also the Ministerial Champion for tackling violence against women and girls overseas, a role that she has held since 2015. She was formerly a Government Whip and spokesperson for the Cabinet Office, International Development and Equalities and Women's Issues. In 2018, Baroness Verma became Chair of the UN Women National Committee UK.

She was made a Conservative life peer on 2 June 2006, taking the title Baroness Verma of Leicester in the County of Leicestershire.

"I was left inspired by Sandip. Her energy and passion is contagious and I admire her for standing up to the gender inequality that exists in our world today."

ANITA GOYAL

I always find myself being very reflective, and the first time I went to Amritsar after I became a member of the House of Lords, my breath was taken away by the beautiful building and magnificent temple. That a girl who had come from here had managed to crack so many ceilings to get to where she was – maybe the place I started from has helped me shape that because even now when I go there they call me the Daughter of Amritsar, which I am and I am proud to be.

I was nine months old when I came to the United Kingdom from India in 1960. Even now I have a strong affiliation with India as I was born there. My mother went into labour with me in the Golden Temple, also known as Sri Harmandir Sahib or Darbar Sahib, which is a Gurdwara located in the city of Amritsar, Punjab, India. It is the holiest Gurdwara and the most important pilgrimage site of Sikhism, so it's a very special place for me. My father was a customs officer stationed in Amritsar and my mother lived in a home where the owners had not had a girl born for many generations – it had always been boys. So when I was born it seemed as if all the delights that they could have in one go suddenly arrived! Sadly, in our culture, Indian girls are perceived as a burden and here was an elderly couple who just absolutely doted on my coming into the world. I was very lucky as I think I found a really beautiful entry into the world. I think it shapes you, what you experience very early on in life, and conditions you for the rest of your life.

My father went to London first and then my mother joined him back in 1960. When he first arrived in Leicester, he applied for a range of jobs. In spite of being an educated man, he expected to find a job aligned with his level of education, but that was not to be. He wore a turban, as a proud Sikh would, and this may have worked against him. His father had been a captain in the British Army, but none of that mattered anymore – they were on white soil and immigrants were not equal. Once my father got over that, he fitted in really well. He later progressed to trading on market stalls and his hard work and vision led him to open his first factory producing hosiery in 1967. Leicester's industrial wealth was built on three core industries in the 1960s: hosiery, boot and shoe manufacture and engineering, and my father was part of that. All of those things taught us that if you work hard, you can achieve and make money, and money allows you access to all sorts of other things especially when it comes to helping others. I am proud to say that my mother and father have embraced British society and have made a positive contribution to it.

There has always been a great community spirit in Leicester and my grandfather had helped about fifty families to settle in the UK. I still remember one particular family who still remain good family friends of ours; they came from Hoshiapur (near Jalandhar in Punjab), where my mother is also from. Even though Sayeed Uncle and his family were Muslim, they adored my mother as their sister all because they originated from the same town. The love between our two families still resides today and it was when I got married that my wedding dress was given to me by Sayeed Uncle's family. Although my parents were both Sikh, I grew up not being told that there was a difference between all of us in terms of religion – I actually grew up not knowing that people were from different faiths. They were brown and looked like me and that was it; that was how I was raised.

I was sixteen when I returned to India in my summer holidays and this is where I was to meet my future husband. Ashok lived in Delhi and he was really excited about showing me around this vast bustling city. I called him Uncle at that time because there is an eleven-year gap between us. During our trip I can recall myself thinking that he was rather arrogant and I didn't particularly like him. He was, in Indian terms a good-looking chap, fair-skinned, tall and slim. An ideal man who everybody wanted their daughter to marry. But he was to be mine. The following year, Ashok came to England, he stayed with us and he got on exceptionally well with my parents. Before I knew it, they all agreed that he was an ideal match for me! I was only seventeen years old, in the middle of studying for my 'A' levels and I was to marry this man who I hardly knew. I was angry that I had to stop studying, but that was the way it was in those days. It was normal and no one really questioned it. When I married Ashok, I discovered that he was a wonderful man and he fully encouraged me to carry on with my studies. He is always fascinated by my thoughts and has always cheered me on to do whatever I wanted. He is my biggest champion and the best companion that I could ever have.

I married into a Hindu family and very quickly I learnt about the numerous traditions that encapsulated the family. As a child, my mother would tell me stories of Lord Krishna and Lord Shiva and that was all I knew about Hinduism. I was immersed into a new world where my mother-in-law was conventionally traditional. After our wedding, I moved in with Ashok, his parents and four brothers-in-law. On our wedding night, my husband asked me, "What gift can I give you?" I responded by saying, "I am really political and at some point in my lifetime I would like to take up politics actively." This was a conversation we were having on our wedding night, which is a bit bizarre especially as you are getting to know someone. My father-in-law was a great man, he told everyone firmly that "Sandip is a child and nobody is to upset her, everyone is to make her happy." That made all the difference. I was valued and adored by this wonderful new family. I would play football in the park with my younger brothers-in-law and I was aware that the neighbours were surprised by this. Is this the way that daughters-in-law should be behaving? I was fortunate, as I had an adorable father-in-law where we would have long meaningful conversations full of fun and laughter. It is rare to have a father-in-law that helps his daughter-in-law recognise her self-worth and value. Totally unconventional for Asian families, even today. However, as a headstrong young ambitious female in the house, if I had something to say, I always shared it directly with the person as opposed to gossiping. These men, along with my husband, have helped shape me into who I am today. It was very sad when my father and father-in-law passed away within six months of each other. The affection that I shared with both of them was very special.

But some are not so lucky. I was in my early twenties when I encountered the real pain of a female who suffered terribly at the hands of domestic violence. She had been brutally thrown out of a bedroom window by her husband who had tried to disfigure her. He wanted to disfigure her because she was an attractive young lady and he wasn't good looking. It was an arranged marriage, he knew that he was marrying an attractive woman and his complex plagued his thinking. We had to defend and support her, assisting her through the court system. Sadly, the court process wasn't sympathetic – they were harsh and that, coupled with a vicious Asian community and family, made her life hell. That experience taught me a lot about the rights of women and I became a standard bearer, so the people of Leicester knew that if there were any issues around that, they knew which door to knock on. I found some brilliant women to work with and the great thing about this is that together we can find a solution. More recently, I helped a woman who suffered domestic violence for several years. She's a mother of three daughters and she had put up with the abuse for many years until her husband had started to hit the girls. At that point I think she decided enough was enough and this was the defining moment in her life when she knew she had to take action against this man. My advice to other women in this situation is that, *you must always remember you are not alone. There will always be somebody who will help you and hold your hand.*

When David Cameron became Prime Minister in 2010, he appointed me as his global champion for tackling violence against women and girls across the globe. This enabled me to talk at government level about what countries do, how we could work together, how we could identify that there is an issue and how we get institutions to be much more responsive in tackling it. There are so many issues in our country – two women every week are killed by partners or husbands. This is an alarming figure and more needs to be done about tackling violence against women. So why do I keep getting up in the morning feeling passionate about making a difference? Who will inspire the next group of people to take up the mantle because this is an issue that is not going to be dealt with in a few years? It is going to be generational, people are going to have to keep doing a little bit every time, every generation. The platform of being in the House of Lords gives me a huge privilege and allows me access to places that normally, even if you do brilliant work, you may not get admittance to.

There are so many inequalities that have infuriated me and I can specifically recall when I was in hospital, nearly nineteen years old and had just given birth to my first child – a beautiful daughter. Next to me in the hospital bed was a young Muslim girl and she had given birth to her son. She turned towards me and shared, "I am so glad I had a son because if I had not had a son they were not going to take me home." I held my daughter in my arms thinking it was the most fantastic thing ever on the planet. She then said to me, "Is your husband going to be alright?" I just couldn't register why she was saying what she did, until I realised that there are still families today who just despise the fact that you have had a daughter! Then later that day, I had a visitor who came to see me. She was very old-fashioned; she had travelled somewhere from the West Midlands and she simply said, "Never mind, next time!" I was disgusted and I actually asked my husband to show her out. It was my moment of happiness, I didn't need someone to spoil it. That attitude is still alive and kicking today but these nuggets that come into your life really do harden you.

I had to be tough as a child growing up in Leicester. I remember my earliest encounter with racism was when I was at school with my step-aunt. We were six months apart in age and we were the only two brown faces in the whole school. Throughout my school days, I grew up being called all sorts of names where one day everybody is your friend and the next day everybody is not your friend. This made relationships very questionable, so I grew up with that, doubting friendships. I remember the second time that someone had an issue with my skin colour – a family friend's daughter pointed out the darkness of my skin and stated, "Don't wash your hands in my sink because you will make my sink dirty!" I was really hurt by that, especially because she was also Asian. Can you imagine a five-year-old having that imprinted in their mind? It stayed with me and I just felt that here were people that were going to judge you because of the colour of your skin, whereas I grew up in a family where no one mentioned colour. My mother was fair-skinned, my father was dark-skinned. I happen to take after my father and though we didn't see it as an issue, those sorts of experiences outside the family start to shape how you see the world. I discovered as a child that you have to go out into the world and live a double life, where there is the Indian in you that you need to maintain because your family expects it at home, but at the same time you have got to navigate yourself within the Western culture. But what this Indian young woman said to me when I was five did matter, and now I fight so hard on the grounds of race in this country because it is impregnated into my brain that people are quite horrible to you if you don't fit a particular colour.

I was only thirteen years old when the National Front (NF) started in Leicester and I was attending the worst school ever in the city, on an estate where there were lots of people supporting the NF. The NF is a far-right, fascist political party in the UK and it was a frightening time for me, and again, remember, not many people looked like me so I faced a choice: am I going to stand up and fight or am I going to be made to be frightened? My father had one principle in life about fright, he said "Never come home crying," which therefore meant that you stood up and fought or you couldn't go home crying. That was the problem, where do you go? I decided to stand up for myself, being much tougher than most people are today. I am still incredibly tough and can take a lot of things; I have a very high threshold of being able to take a lot of stress before it gets to me.

At school I was a bright girl, highly academic and always in the top three so I was on the right side of the teachers. I wouldn't tolerate bullying of any kind in the school and again I was a leader of my classmates. I always stood up for the person that everybody else didn't like; people would pick on them, but not on my watch. I think, in your head you have this internal justice system going on so you can see right and wrong, and I have never feared a challenge. In the school play, I wanted to know why we couldn't have Snow Black – Snow White was there so why couldn't I become a lead? You throw things out there to see what happens and if they can't change the title then they can change the story. I was a challenger and I have always been a disrupter.

There is one thing that I will keep asking questions about, and that is what happened at the Jallianwala Bagh massacre which took place on 13 April 1919 when troops of the British Indian Army, under the command of Colonel Reginald Dyer, fired rifles into a crowd of unarmed Indians. Why did this happen? The peaceful crowd gathered at the ceremonial ground near the Golden Temple on the day of Bhaisakhi – one of the largest spring festivals of the Sikh community. It has been on my conscience for as long as I can remember, and every time I visit it, I still feel the eeriness of the people that died there. I think there is an important question to be answered. These were defenceless men, women and children killed and wounded ruthlessly. I will always ask that question, I don't want big enquiries or apologies because history is done. I just want to know why somebody took the decision to open fire on innocent people who had no guns and no armoury. In the centenary of this massacre, we need to know the lessons from it so we don't do it again. Now why do I ask that? Our history should reflect what we know, and as a proud Sikh, Hindu and Indian, all of those things I am extremely proud about because I think it is easier to airbrush everything out if you really don't like it. There are some horrific things that go on in India but I come from there, and whilst I am a really proud British citizen loving this country, I think there are questions that need to be answered in order for people to move on. My curiosity tells me that the decision may have come from the UK. Or was it someone in India who decided to play a power game because they could? What can the Indians in India learn from poor power games? Politics everywhere is going downhill and it matters to me especially.

I think if you don't like the status quo you shake it up and you disrupt, especially if it negates the strength and potential of people simply because of where they are born, who they are born to, what they look like, the colour of their skin or their gender. If it stops you from being able to be the best that you are in whatever field then we need to disrupt it.

If I have wanted to do something, I have not waited for somebody to tell me to do it, I have just gone and done it and if I fail at it, at least I tried. I am not frightened of failure and five years ago, my son shared a great lesson with me. He said, "You know what, Mum, one thing I learned was failure is not that bad." Actually, he is right – failure is not bad, it just gives you an opportunity to reassess. My children have been brilliant, they have known a mum who is constantly on the go. They have never put demands on me. Occasionally they say, "We would quite like this, would you mind cooking it for us?" but apart from that my son and daughter have been really flexible and have observed that their mum can make a difference. I believe that this has inspired them to go on and actually make a difference to other people's lives. I constantly have to touch my head and say I am really lucky. It has been painful on the way – I have had lots of negative people confront me on the way, people who feel they should be the obstacle rather than somebody to assist me on my journey. But I still made it and they are still waiting, and they can keep waiting because I believe that if you are full of that much jealousy or lack of your own self-belief then you don't deserve to be at the front. People who go out there without any malice for anybody else deserve to be at the front.

One of my greatest accomplishments is my position as Chair of United Nations (UN) Women UK. I am hugely passionate about this planet and climate change and believe the biggest impact will be in 2050 when we will have 9 billion people on the planet – we are going to have a shortage of food and water. I have spent the last three years of this decade preparing myself, and opportunities aligned with my vision have landed in my lap. UN Women UK came on that journey, I didn't seek it out. I will utilise this platform to raise awareness of issues that matter to me. The privilege of having such influence is to utilise it to make changes. My next decade is going to be much more about the planet, more about how I can positively affect change. Younger people are talking much more about self-preservation. This gorgeous land that has been bestowed upon us – it's my time to do something about it.

I pinch myself when I am walking into the House of Lords, thinking, *God, the people that have walked here before me.* That still amazes me, the fact that I have done it. I appreciate where I came from and know where I'm going.

Ashok and Sandip – engagement ceremony

Sandip's father and mother

SEVEN

Witness to a Life
LADY MOHINI KENT NOON

Lady Mohini Kent Noon is an author, filmmaker, journalist and charity worker. A student of yoga philosophy, she views life as a journey of consciousness, to be fully explored and realised. She has written books and plays, directed stage productions and films, and gives public talks on various issues that reflect her wide range of interests. She was married to the late Lord Noon and now lives alone in London.

"The Hemraj Goyal Foundation have been supporting the charity LILY Against Human Trafficking since being inspired by Lady Noon in 2014. The relationship between the two charities has gone from strength to strength and the number of girls and women that have been impacted through the projects has risen too."

ANITA GOYAL

The two most important events for a human being are birth and death, and I was born in Amritsar. What we make of the time in between the two events is a mixture of freewill, karmic baggage and personal struggle. London was to become my home, even though my childhood homes were firmly located in Delhi, Lucknow and Jullundur, with family, gymkhana clubs, mango trees, *litchi* and *jamun* trees, heat, dust-storms, Irish nuns and a world that vanished so quickly that it seems but a dream. As John Lennon said: "Life is what happens to you while you're busy making other plans."

My mother was taken for her accouchement to Amritsar to the home of the then Guru of the Radha Soami sect, who was a close family friend. I believe it was an old-fashioned house with high ceilings, and one afternoon when my mother should have been resting in the bedroom but was elsewhere, a large concrete ornament detached itself from the ceiling and crashed on the empty bed. My story could have ended even before it began.

My grandmother belonged to an Amritsar family and her ancestors were given the title of *masadis* to the holy shrine by the gurus. As a girl, she bathed at dawn in the '*amrit sarovar*' (sea of nectar), and they named my mother Amrit. Guru Arjan Dev, who built the Harmandir Sahib, fifth in the line of the ten gurus, invited a Muslim, Mian Mir, to lay its foundation stone, and he opened it to the four castes of Hinduism by constructing four doors. With this background, it seemed incumbent on me to embrace all religions, and I am a Sikh, a Hindu, a Buddhist, a Sufi and even a little bit Christian.

My grandmother left her home in 1921 to marry Kanwar Madanjeet Singh of Kapurthalla, one of the five Sikh kingdoms of Punjab, the others being Patiala, Nabha, Jind and Faridkot. Indian families traditionally left no room for individuality, especially for women. She, a simple teenager, was yoked to a man fresh from the Sandhurst Military Academy in England. I believe he was an aide-de-camp to King George V before returning home. A gulf separated husband and wife, a gulf of education, taste, preferences, gambling, three kitchens, seventy-five servants and even the British Empire. He ordered his clothes from Jermyn Street in London, his cut-glass-and-silver toilette set from Dunhill, and he enjoyed gambling. My grandmother retained her Amritsar roots. She also found herself in *purdah* (veiled from male eyes, including servants and the public). Even Kanwarani Madanjeet Singh's Daimler car and railway saloon had curtains, and the doctor felt her pulse through a curtain. Shopping was left to *munshis* – clerks – so they were royally cheated out of everything, including jewels. Things changed with his premature death in 1932, and his family descended to strip her of whatever they could; families of rich men feed like vultures on the widow after his death.

Decades later, over dinner at the Sandhurst Academy, the Commandant invited me to see their old records, and also shared that Ian Fleming, creator of James Bond, was at Sandhurst in 1917. Since Kanwar Madanjeet Singh too was there in 1917–18, they would have been acquainted.

My mother was saved from a cloistered existence by being sent away to boarding school in Lahore. Queen Mary's was an upper crust establishment for girls of royal families from all over India. Miss Cox, their English headmistress, taught them the Queen's English, ballroom dancing, deportment, swimming, and Urdu was also taught as a concession to Lahore. My mother went on to become an Urdu scholar and poet, wrote plays in Urdu and books in English, sang on stage and made records. She played tennis, went swimming with us and studied Ikebana, the Japanese art of flower arranging, and I remember her thematic creations: War and Peace and Anna Karenina. The Partition of India separated my mother from her Muslim school friends left behind in Pakistan.

The English were virtually unique in partitioning the lands of their empire before departing, as compared to the Portuguese, French, Spanish and Dutch. The Partition of India followed an imperial policy of divide and rule based on ignorance of the ancient Indian philosophy, culture and ethos. Back home in Britain, everyone was Christian, the religion of Europe was Christianity and the divisions were sectarian. The English rulers lacked the intellectual depth to understand Hinduism and Islam, deemed them to be inferior to Christianity and created divisions. Partition was a dishonourable act in a long British imperial tale of blood and treachery. No proper announcement was made, and even the boundaries were announced two days after 15 August by Radcliffe, a man who had no knowledge of India, its religions or cultures. The severe traumas suffered by Indians have lived in families down the generations and across the world in migrations to Commonwealth countries, America and Europe. In my latest novel, *Black Taj*, Simi's grandmother, Old Mrs Bhandari, cannot forgive and forget the loss suffered by her father because of the violent partition, when the family wealth was wiped away overnight. *Black Taj* is a love story set against the background of class and conflict in modern India, and the fabled Taj Mahal. In 1993, when the Babri Mosque crumbles, so does Simi's life. To the horror of her grandmother and the outrage of their friends in the riot-torn city of Atmapuri, she, a Hindu girl, falls deeply in love with an unsuitable Muslim doctor. But the ghost of Partition stands between the lovers. What will be their fate? India has welcomed all faiths, is a natural spiritual home for all, and that's her unique contribution to the world, but religion has created more conflict than any other issue.

Eye witnesses to the brutality can best convey the devastation that Mountbatten and Clement Attlee unleashed on India by giving less than three months' notice for the exchange of populations, let alone sale of property and business. My sister Keku lives in New York with her husband, Dr Harish Moorjani, whose father Kishen was fourteen in 1947 and a resident of Sindh, now in Pakistan. The Sindhi Moorjani family lived in an ordinary middle-class locality that was seized by a Muslim named Mir, who had moved from Delhi in those turbulent days. Mir desisted from killing the family only because he had promised his Sikh friend in Delhi to spare lives and instead send people across to him. So he offered the Moorjanis an escort of three men on the train to Delhi. Kishen had been a boy scout and that connection proved vital. His 'scout master' obtained a permit from the Deputy Commissioner of Hyderabad, with the all-important official seal, for the scout and his family of six to travel. His mother sold her one remaining gold bangle to purchase tickets for the family. They boarded the train for Delhi at Hyderabad, Sindh, but nobody knew where the border was because it had not been announced. At one of the last junctions before Delhi, the lights went out and a mob boarded the dark train armed with knives, guns and machetes. They went through the compartments, hacking passengers to death along the way. The agonised screams of the dying and the stench of blood was unbearable, and the now eighty-five-year-old Kishen, who lives in New Jersey, still suffers from nightmares.

The petrified Moorjani family huddled in a corner of the railway coach, waiting for certain death. But when the mob reached them their escort did not run away. Astonishingly, Mir's three men stood by them, and pointed out that the Moorjani family had official government protection. The mob leader examined the document by the light of his torch, then shone it on their faces one by one. Somehow, he was prevailed upon to honour the official seal and he spared their lives. The mob went on to butcher the remaining passengers. Through the window of the train, Kishen witnessed the murders on the platform. He saw a pregnant woman being knifed to death, other women raped and killed, and Sikhs and Hindus savagely attacked with machetes, knives and daggers. The ferocity was mindboggling and the horror of what he had seen was impossible to forget, and has stayed with him over the decades. The trauma and anxiety was even communicated to his children, born long after the event. At least his story had a happy ending. The terrified family arrived at Old Delhi Railway Station and made their way to the Sikh gentleman, Mir's friend, who gave them a room to live in. Later, Kishen miraculously met up with his older brother who had left home much earlier. In 1947 they had no phones and the postal service was disrupted, so each had no idea if the other was still alive. Then they found their eldest brother in a Calcutta lunatic asylum. He had signed up to the British Army and left home to fight on the Western Front in World War II. After witnessing the horrors of that war he had lost his mental balance and was sent to the asylum. In India, about 16 million people migrated on both sides during Partition, and about 1 million died.

On 13 April 1919, the Amritsar massacre took place when my paternal grandfather, Shamsher Singh Kent, was still a medical student in Lahore. General Dyer ordered the firing and more than 1,500 unarmed Sikh men, women and children were injured by 1,600 bullets in Jallianwala Bagh, an enclosed space in which they were trapped. About 1,000 were killed. At first the House of Lords applauded General Dyer. The brutality of the English rulers stunned the Indians. My grandfather, a turbaned Sikh, raised a petition against the massacre. The racist English principal of his medical college quietly removed him from that institution. Instead, Shamsher Singh applied and was accepted at medical college in England, and sailed from the Bombay Docks in 1918. In Liverpool, he fell in love with his English landlady's daughter, but was prevented from marrying her by his perceptive mother who sent him the traditional telegram that read: *Mother very ill. Return immediately*. He returned home and became the first Indian medical officer on the British Indian Railways. My father, Tej Pratap Singh Kent, universally known as Patty, was raised in an anglicised household, and studied at Sherwood boarding school in Nainital. High-spirited, with a keen sense of humour, he was a devoted father who made our childhood fun, dressing up as Father Christmas, arranging treasure hunts at our birthday parties, playing board games with us on winter nights and even cooking breakfast on Sundays. He taught us by example the values of honesty, straightforwardness, punctuality and decency. His friends describe him as being "as straight as a knife". Lying or cheating was anathema to him. A dedicated sportsman, he took us swimming, played tennis and badminton, and encouraged me to join the school hockey team and become the school sports captain. But his real worth emerged when he suffered a crippling stroke at the age of sixty, which left him disabled. Suddenly he, an athlete who had not spent even a night in hospital, was trapped in a body that did not function normally. Even his speech was affected, making conversation difficult. At first, he became intensely angry and frustrated, and it took him some years to replace these feelings with an unflagging cheerfulness, which welled up from deep within him. His tremendous courage in facing life as a disabled person, with his right side paralysed, unable to read or write, was the greatest lesson for me. From being a highly educated technocrat, a mechanical engineer, widely travelled, with beautiful handwriting that I emulated, he was reduced to fumbling for words, unable to converse or walk properly. Gradually, friends and relatives dropped off. As Kafka wrote in *Metamorphosis*, at first everyone is intensely concerned, but over a period of time they become indifferent. The family is forced to come to terms with the sadness. The world goes its merry way.

When I moved to London, I thought it would be like an extension of Delhi. I had studied in Loreto and Carmel convent schools, and been raised by educated and urbane parents. Indian convent schools were, up until the 1970s, overtly Catholic, with scripture lessons, the Lord's Prayer, biblical films and Christmas collections. But all that has changed in India now and they include prayers from Indian faiths and celebrate other sacred days as well.

London was a totally unexpected experience. I found a reserved race, and the climate was even colder. But as I became a Londoner I grew to appreciate its grand museums and civilised ways. I enjoy walking in Regent's Park and watching the swans and ducks, and wonder why they say crazy as a coot! I studied graphics at Middlesex Polytechnic, after obtaining a first-class degree in Psychology from Delhi's Lady Shri Ram College, and went on to learn filmmaking on Wardour

Street. I feel I have led five lives in one, having worked as a journalist, film director, playwright and author. And no matter what else I did, I continued doing charitable work over the decades. It worried me that I was doing too many things until I put the question to Sri MP Pandit of Sri Aurobindo Ashram, Pondicherry, where I do regular spiritual retreats. He replied that it was a sign of expanded consciousness and nothing to worry about. Sri Aurobindo wrote: "The world is other than we now think and see; Our lives a deeper mystery than we have dreamed." "All Life is Yoga," he said, and that we have to meet the challenges of daily life with a spiritual attitude.

India is rich in epics, and the *Ramayana* is one of the most beloved. It has incredible plots and stories, and I began reading versions of it as a student. Then I wrote a script for a feature-length production which I directed on stage. Prince Charles attended the premiere in London, and the musical production toured Britain and India. The *Ramayana* is a love story, and a tale of courage and chivalry. Lord Rama had a difficult life, and our production too became mired in difficulties, including the overnight disappearance of our lead actor who played Rama. He betrayed the fifty-strong team, but the show went on. Sita, despite being born a princess and destined to become queen, was an abused woman. She was exiled by the king, her husband, to satisfy public opinion, and that's after she had undertaken the fire ordeal to prove her innocence. It was too late when he tried to get her back after many years, and she chose to merge with the earth and disappear.

Oscar-winning actor Sir Ben Kingsley did the English commentary for my *Ramayana* film, based on the stage production. It was like a masterclass to work with Sir Ben, and he was very friendly. Later, when he happened to be in Delhi at the same time, I took him and his wife to Chandni Chowk, to the silver market and the old eateries. He also came to watch a play that my mother wrote in which we all acted, and that may be the only time an Oscar-winning actor watched a small stage production in Delhi.

Sir Ben also did the English commentary for my documentary film, *Curry Tiffin*, on the history of India through food. I wrote and directed the film, a gastronomical journey through Hindu food, the Moghul kitchens and the clubs of the British Raj, and research for the script threw up nuggets such as the anecdote that the 'Punch' cocktail was inspired by '*Panchamrit*', a sacred liquid of five ingredients such as milk, yoghurt and honey used in temples to bathe deities and later distributed to devotees. The Moghul emperors ate only in the harem because of a very real threat of poisoning. Imperial cooks would prepare one hundred dishes for the emperor's every meal, and dishes were locked and sealed in the kitchen. The seal was broken in the emperor's presence when a food taster sampled everything. The harem could be a township of about 5,000, including the royal women, concubines, maids, dancing girls, eunuchs and female guards. I shot the film on location in Delhi, Lucknow, Banaras and Calcutta, and met many interesting people along the way. The old Maharaja of Banaras, HH Vibhuti Narain Singh, was a gentle, kindly man, and I had tea with him alone a few times on his palace balcony under which flowed the holy river Ganges.

India is the world's biggest food bazaar. There are those who eat wheat and others who eat only rice, those who cook in ghee (clarified butter) and others who cook in coconut oil. Northerners drink tea from Darjeeling, but in the South they drink coffee from Coorg. Annapoorna is the Hindu Goddess of Food, and food acquires great ritual significance in a Hindu's life and death, when offerings are made to the departed soul. The Maharaja of Banaras drank only Ganges water. The teachings of the Buddha highlighted compassion and that gave the impetus to vegetarianism. Sikh gurudwaras offer free food to all, irrespective of caste or creed. The last invaders of India, after the Greeks, Turks, Arabs, Moghuls, Portuguese and French, were the English. They came looking for spices but stayed on to conquer India. The legendary maharajas were epicures and fabulous hosts, employing dozens of master chefs who specialised in just one dish. They were also keen patrons of Cartier's jewels and Rolls-Royce cars. Now that cultures are mixed, curry is a British national dish, and Moghlai food is an international taste.

As a student in London I was introduced to the writings of Mevlana Jalaluddin Rumi, although Sufism is part of my Sikh heritage, and in 2007 UNESCO Year of Rumi my mother and I collaborated on a play on the great Sufi mystic. Our production, titled *Rumi: Unveil the Sun*, was performed to critical acclaim both in London and in Delhi, where it won theatre awards. Through intense suffering, Rumi was transformed into a mystic from a cleric, and the power and truth of his spiritual realisation is such that, 800 years after his birth, his poetry and books are widely read in translation all over the world.

Rumi's teachings have continued to influence me at critical moments. I've had many Masters, many Guides, all of whom have told me to look up and exceed my human limitations. It is the natural tendency of the Indian mind to seek the companionship of God. HH Dalai Lama teaches compassion and to be joyful in all circumstances, and he has given the Foreword to my book on Nagarjuna, also known as the Second Buddha. The Dalai Lama writes that he recites a verse from Nagarjuna's writings as soon as he wakes up, which is in praise of the Buddha and his explanation of emptiness.

Our beautiful world is stocked with dazzling objects, but it's also a hard school. My latest charity, LILY Against Human Trafficking, is named after a four-year-old girl who was sold into sex slavery for about £50. I discovered the heartbreaking world of human slavery after having done voluntary work in education and health for almost thirty years. Today, the trade in human beings is worth an estimated 100 billion dollars. My charity LILY helps to run schools and educational initiatives, sheltered homes, employment schemes and anything and everything we can do to fight the evil trade.

Lily was just four, an age of innocence and purity, when she was imprisoned in a Delhi brothel, being raped by adult men. She was rescued and grew up in a sheltered home we supported. When she completed school at eighteen, we asked her what was her life's ambition. Did she dream of becoming a doctor, a lawyer, an airhostess, a businesswoman, or just rich and famous? None of those, it transpired. She burst into tears and said, "I want to teach mothers to love their children. My mother did not love me otherwise she would not have sold me." For the truth is that Lily was sold by her own mother, a prostitute dependent on alcohol and drugs to numb her feelings as she survived in the brutal world of prostitution.

I ran a campaign in a British Indian newspaper for a year for which I wrote the tragic stories of real girls with real lives who live in the dark and violent world of child prostitution. Haima was thirteen and already the mother of a boy when she was trafficked from the holy city of

Banaras and brought to Delhi. She was sold to a brothel, and her baby boy was sold separately to a couple. Radha was fourteen, and from a poor family from Rajasthan, when she was tricked and sold to a brothel, where she was beaten and starved into obedience. The choice was stark: comply or forfeit her life. The first case I heard of was of a tiny girl of three being sold to a brothel. When she was rescued, she was five, and soon died from internal injuries.

I am always shocked by how little it costs to buy a human being. And astounded by how easy it is to ignore the whole issue; it seems possible for people to be shocked and bored at the same time. There are an estimated 2 to 3 million children in brothels in India alone. We cannot look the other way because we all are, each one of us, part of the human race, of the same collective energy. None of us will be free until we free the very last slave. Human intelligence has built wonders in space and in the oceans and on land. Now we must, with compassion and ethics, end the agony of the poor, the exploited, the enslaved. I feel that I've been working in charity all my life. When I was about eleven, I gave my weekly pocket money to our cook, Jagata, whose children I was very fond of. We lived in Lucknow at the time, and my father was trying to teach me to handle money but there was nothing I wanted to buy. Through my earlier charity, Parbati Foundation, I focused on education and health, and LILY works against human trafficking. The work has taught me humility and empathy, and to love without judgement. These girls did not choose that life.

Women, in particular, are most at risk. Apart from physical enslavement in brothels, even well-to-do women are disempowered by families, especially husbands.

Women have to claim their freedom, even educated women. Economic freedom is a big step. For a poor and illiterate woman, it is impossible to find freedom without help. I have been fighting against barriers imposed on women through power and control, particularly in the Indian culture. My charity is an expression of that. Women are taught to think about their bodies, thoughts and emotions in a particular way. Some barriers are self-imposed and we can become prisoners of our own mentality. I wanted to exceed myself, to study, work, write, paint, meditate, meet spiritual guides and explore my consciousness, so that's what I did.

Increasingly I ask myself, why am I here, what's the purpose of it all? A few things that I've learnt along the way are: women must claim their freedom; going beyond fear is the key; stick to the truth, even when others succeed better in the world by dubious means; be true to yourself even if you're mocked for being unworldly; be kind to yourself and take care of your body; be compassionate to others; acquire knowledge; seek the Divine every day in a very personal and urgent way.

*Mohini's grandmother Kanwarani Madanjeet Singh (left), of the royal
Kapurthalla State, and Mohini's mother, Amrit (married to Patty Kent)*

Mohini with her mother and sister

Mohini with HH Dalai Lama (Raj Thakkar of Expressions)

*Mohini's Ramayana dance-drama – a royal premiere with
HRH Prince Charles*

EIGHT

Sorority Girl

KULJIT KAUR SHARMA

Dressed as a boy at a young age was how Kuljit's father designed her childhood. He was an advocate for all children to have gender equality. He wanted his daughters to have the same rights and opportunities in civil society and be able to contribute in an equal way without discrimination. He instilled values and beliefs that were ahead of his time to serve his country. Kuljit was part of a sorority of modern, educated women at her university and on British soil she encountered challenges and hardship – eventually losing her identity of being a phenomenal headteacher in Punjab. This is the story of a woman that gave up so much to be in Britain with her loving husband.

ANITA GOYAL

I was born in 1933. My name is Kuljit Sharma and I am eighty-five years old. There is a place called Barnala in Punjab. When I was born, my father was stationed there as a Tehsildaar (Executive Magistrate of the Tehsil, or administrative division). He was transferred around India a lot; still, my childhood was a happy one.

I was fourteen years old during the Partition of India. Everyone was afraid of everyone else. There were a thousand stories of girls being kidnapped and tortured, so everyone was tense lest it happened to their own. But as far as I am aware, this was the story of some, not most. Those who wanted to go to Pakistan went and lived just as they had in India, and vice versa. But again, that was the story of most; some were not so lucky. Sometimes, trains came into India from Pakistan full of sick, injured and even tortured Hindus who had got in the way of one Muslim or another. When they came on the trains, the Indians took care of them. There was fighting, from both sides. People thought badly of those coming from the other side; they were refugees and constrained to the camps until the Government began to help them. They formed the Rehabilitation Department and facilitated the settlement of the new arrivals. I am proud to share that my father was a rehabilitation officer.

Some of the Indian people were hesitant to go to Pakistan; they knew nothing of that place. My father formed the Consolidation Mehakama, which is a council or court. It arranged safe passage for girls to travel across the newly formed border, the Radcliffe Line. My father used to tell us stories of the people in the camps. A large part of his job was to interview them about themselves. Based on what they told him, they were supported through their rehabilitation. He once told us of some Muslim girls who were afraid to make the journey to Pakistan. My father gathered them up, arranged for a lorry and sent them safely on their way. As I remember it, they were sent to a Pakistani state called Malerkotla. They were safe.

My mother and father were married for thirteen years or so before they were finally bestowed with a child; it was my grand entry into this world! My mother wanted a son, but she had a daughter, and then eventually my sister. My father was always of the opinion that the education of girls was more important than that of boys. I grew up in an era where girls in Punjab were generally not allowed to study or even go out for that matter. We were raised as boys, dressed as boys. This was my father's way of protecting us.

My father would say, "There is no difference. It is one family whether it is girls or boys, all are good."

We also had an older sister, a child from my father's first marriage. Unfortunately, my father's first wife died and when he got re-married, my mother brought the child up as her own daughter. We call her Prakash Bhan ji. Further along the way, my dear brother was born.

One initiative that came out of the Consolidation Department my father formed ensured equal rights for all genders. At the time, girls didn't even have rights over family property but his department changed this. For example, if in a family there were four children made up of two daughters and two sons, this resulted in four equal shares of the property. The boarding school I went to was called Sikh Kanya Vidyalaya. I don't know if it still stands, that land is now in Pakistan. There were only a handful of girls in the school. Whether you were rich or poor, no one sent their girls out unprotected. I guess you'd call them bodyguards these days; we called that common sense.

I then continued to study at the Punjab University for my degree. There were eight girls and the rest were boys, all of whom attended Ranbir College, which was affiliated with Punjab University. After about ten years, by the time my brother started going to the school, there were almost fifty girls. The college started to flourish where more and more girls sought admission. However, when I was still there, they separated the boys from the girls – separate rooms, separate facilities. There was a lawn where we sat in the sunlight every day and even that was separate for the girls. Naturally, we did not mix much, but I do remember that the girls were given priority to access better facilities. Some boys used to object to this, saying, "We have paid the same fee as the girls. Why are we not treated the same way?" Our lecturers would usually reply, saying, "If your own sisters were studying here, how would you feel then?"

Like I said, we didn't mix much but when we did, we did so hesitantly. For example, we had launched a magazine and that was a collaborative effort. It was called *Jyoti* and we were very proud of it. It was circulated both in school and out of school. I was the second editor so rather than write articles, I supported the other girls with their work and checked it. So, suppose someone – particularly a boy – wanted to ask something or wanted to submit an article to the magazine, then they approached girls, tentatively. I remember a young man called Prem Sharma; he never met a girl without backup. Whenever he came to ask us something, he would walk timidly over to the girls and say politely, "We are doing this and would like to contribute this. How can we help, how would you do it?"

I studied History, Economics and English as one had to study three subjects for a degree. When I finished, I told my father I wanted to do Prabhakar. Prabhakar is the highest degree in Hindi. Very few people studied it, even fewer of them women.

I bought the guides and prepared for it; a Pundit ji would come and tutor me in Sanskrit, which is the classical language of India and the liturgical language of Hinduism, Buddhism and Jainism. It is also one of the twenty-two official languages of India. My father had arranged that for me, but then again, that was my norm because my father arranged every request I made. I was very lucky growing up.

I was appointed to teach in a girls' high school, on the basis of the Prabhakar. While I was posted there I worked as a headmistress too. My second degree was in Hindi and Sanskrit, and I had a wonderful opportunity to teach the students these two incredible languages until I got married.

In those days, the girls respected the teachers a lot. Where there were two teachers standing together in discussion, no one would pass in front of them. Since I had worked in the same school as a headmistress, I was shown added respect. I used to give a lecture for about an hour on how the girls should behave with their parents, their neighbours and other students through compassion and kindness. It wasn't just me, there was another teacher, Harinder Kaur, who used to give the lectures too. I used to say, "Work is Worship, Rest is Worse."

It means that it is good to work. But to rest, to stay idle, is not good in life. We used to say this even when there was a wedding or celebration.

I got married in Moga, which is a city in the Indian state of Punjab. Moga was named after Moga Singh Gill, a prominent person of the Gill community. Moga is a popular spot for travelling to Lahore. People came by train to Moga and, after that, people travelled to Lahore (now in Pakistan) via buses. Shortly after, I stayed in Bombay for three to four years, working as a teacher while my husband studied for his law degree. My eldest daughter, Sushma, was born in Dhuri in Punjab and in those days it was customary to give birth at your parents' home. My son, Sunny, was also born in Dhuri.

When my husband came to England, I joined him a year later. I remember it well – 13 September 1964. We lived in Bradford as that's where my husband's uncle was staying. Initially, I felt as if I had arrived in a village because the other Indians in the neighbourhood had come from a rural background. Few people were educated and their mindset was very different to mine. I had to adjust a lot to fit in. People used to use a public bath in those days and it was conventional for people to queue up and have a bath once a week. I found that particularly difficult. When we got our own house, I spoke to my husband and told him that I couldn't use a public bath. Our entire house was £350 and we spent £100 on fitting a new bathroom which included a toilet. People were astonished that we did this. But, it was my wish and my husband and I worked to have this little luxury in our lives.

I wanted to be a teacher again, as I had been in India. The rules were different here in the United Kingdom and I would need to do a three-year course to re-train. I did eventually become a teacher, but sadly it wasn't anything like the experience I had in India – I did not like it. The children here thought nothing of teachers; they were so disrespectful, especially towards Asian teachers. There was one boy in particular; I often felt like beating him up! When I was talking to the class, he would sometimes move the bench around, sometimes move the desk and even worse he would bang on it. I hadn't experience of such poor behaviour from students before.

In those days, people didn't have washing machines in their houses. I had gone to wash my clothes at a launderette – the bedsheets and such. This boy that was so disruptive in my class was also there. He started teasing me again, giggling, pointing and just generally being a nuisance. I'd had more than enough of him in school, and now here he was, dancing on my last nerve in broad daylight, while I was just trying to live my life. I don't know what happened to me, but I flipped and grabbed hold of him and slapped him across his face.

He was stunned and once I realised what I'd done, I gave him some money and asked him not to tell. I was sure his mother would arrive at my door, ready to fight me, but no one showed up! I was relieved, to say the least. That did the trick though. He turned into a good boy after that. When I would come from the market after doing my shopping, he would see me on the pavement, greet me and help carry my bags. That boy really did turn himself around. That was just one child.

I had many difficult situations and I really didn't enjoy teaching in British schools. Around noon every day, the children in all the classes were given milk in small glass milk bottles with straws. The milk monitors would come round and deliver the bottles to the younger children and I will never forget when one of the white students asked the other, "How many bottles do you need for Blacky's class?" They were talking about me and I did not like it. I felt terrible, I was being called Blacky! Not even by name – Mrs Sharma. I complained to the headmaster. I said, "Children are being rude to me, how can this be fair?" All I could think about was India, and how different teachers were treated there. In India, of course, the children could still be naughty, but even after I'd punish them they would come and apologise to me and ask that I not report them to their parents. I decided to leave the school after a year and my experience of teaching came to an end in Britain.

My children were young and my husband had his heart set on starting a business so I dropped the idea of teaching, begging him instead to keep his job so that we could still have a steady income. We decided that it would be better that I tried something different, so my husband opened a drapery shop – that is, a shop selling fabrics and sewing materials, children's schoolwear and some fancy goods – and for a while, I managed that. From working there, I learnt that one can do any job, whether big or small. I learnt that a person should be able to adapt themselves to any scenario. Whatever it may be, one should not get nervous. All will fall into place.

Everyone liked to come to our shop. Sometimes, they didn't come to buy anything from me but just to get their papers read. Some of the Asian customers couldn't read or write and I used to fill in their forms and read their papers to them – their income tax forms and that sort of thing. I felt proud. I knew that I was helping people by using my education to do this.

Shortly after, in 1978 we moved to Acton where we bought a shop. It was a grocery shop with an off licence and we were open all hours. In my family, it was not in our values to drink alcohol or smoke cigarettes and this was quite challenging for me, as I now had to sell the stuff. We had to earn a living and if that's what was required then I guess I had no choice. I can share that I learnt that a person should adapt themselves to every scenario. Whatever it may be, one should not get nervous. All will fall into place with time.

There used to be skinheads, a gang that formed in the Southall area, and they used to rob the shops in our area. The skinhead culture originated among working class youths in London, England, in the 1960s and soon spread to other parts of the UK. One day, the skinheads decided to turn their sights to my shop. Luckily for me, however, Mr Patel, from the railways – who often came to my shop for a drink or two – saw ten or twelve of them coming. While they were still on their way, he came running into my shop and frantically proceeded to lock it. At the time, I hadn't the faintest idea what he was doing or why he had closed the door from the inside. He said, "I will tell you, I'll tell you!"

When he was about to tell me, I saw a massive group of people approaching the shop, crossing the bridge before it and walking quickly. My heart was pounding, I was so scared and I had no idea what to do. My daughter Sushma was on her school vacation. She was in the flat upstairs and she had spotted what was happening from our living room window; without hesitation she had already called the police. The skinheads started breaking the windows of my shopfront. It was a very scary experience. The police arrived just in time to arrest many of the thugs! I was saved.

After that – but not because of it – we moved into London and I worked there as an interpreter. I can confidently speak four or five languages, the ones commonly spoken in India: Hindi, Urdu, Punjabi and Sanskrit too. I would be sent to the hospitals and clinics. The nurses would often take me along in their cars. I used to earn ten shillings an hour, so if I worked two hours, that's one pound. The hardship we faced was unenviable as we were the first generation of immigrants from South Asia. We didn't have a lavish lifestyle; we saved to support not only our own children but had to spend money on getting my husband's younger brothers married off too. Being the eldest sister-in-law in the family, it was my ultimate duty to support and arrange the weddings of all three brothers. We didn't order catered food from anywhere; us ladies got together and cooked all the food for all the events in the house. It was the unity and collaboration that bonded us all together and made it so much fun. I would never want anyone to think that I didn't do my bit being the eldest sister-in-law.

Now I am retired. I do find it difficult since my husband passed away. My children help me a lot. They arrive as soon as there is any help needed. My son stays nearby and visits me regularly. Sometimes, he comes in the morning and draws my curtains if I am sleeping.

The thing I think I am most proud of in my life is that I never said no to one in need. I believe that one should do anything one can to help. Furthermore, whatever needs to be done must be done with integrity. Don't be greedy for anything, meaning, *I will do this only if I get this in profit*. If one must help someone, it must be with a pure heart, not in lieu of exchange of benefits. I have tried my best to live like this and teach my children to do the same. My children are very kind and always try their best to help me. Sushma studied very hard to become a pharmacist and she now runs her own business with her husband. My son, Sunny, is a teacher and Head of Science. Teaching these days is so challenging and I'm glad that he has followed in my earlier footsteps. My youngest daughter, Sujata, is an award-winning construction lawyer and a judge. She leads the minority of the top 3% of UK Hindu women working in a predominantly white male-dominated occupation. I am immensely proud of all of my three children as they make such a positive contribution to society and preserve their culture by instilling my teachings in their own children. The future generation are doing even more dynamic things in their lives and they all love me very much.

I am not too concerned about being remembered after I've passed on. What use is praise or reverence to the dead? I try to be a good person while I am alive so that when I'm gone, not a soul will be able to come to my funeral and wish me good riddance. I also don't want to become a burden on my children. At present, that doesn't seem to be the case and I hope it stays that way until I am done with this world of yours.

I am eighty-five years old. This world belongs to the young now. I have nine incredible grandchildren and I'm so proud of all of them. They must live this thing called life for themselves. I am that way with my own children. Even if I come to know something, I don't interfere, you see. I think it is their own life; they are well educated and leaders of their own lives. They should adapt by themselves. I don't have to interfere.

Kuljit (fourth from left) with her classmates

Kuljit dressed as a boy (far right) with her father (seated) – administrator of the Maharaja of Patiala

NINE

The Girl with Auburn Hair
RAJNI KAUL

Dressed in a blue and pink abstract printed long shirt paired with cream trousers, she opened the door of her house for me. There was something so enchanting about her that I could barely greet her. My eyes went straight to her auburn hair, which really stood out. It was only later that I realised I was not the only one who was captivated by this. The energy she emitted at her age was infectious and I was ready to capture as much of it as I could.

AASTHA K SINGHANIA

Our life is a blank canvas and He has left us with all the colours we need with which to fill it. It is for us to decide which colour to use and when. All my life, this belief helped me pull through all these years. My name is Rajni Kaul and I was born in Peshawar on 15 July 1929. When I close my eyes, the first thing that comes to my mind is that five-storey building we lived in and how, as a three-year-old, I had once climbed onto the roof to sit at the edge with my feet dangling in the air. It was scary but the view kept me captivated. I could see Peshawar spread below me. The city felt so far and wide; the breeze wanted to make me jump with it. I wanted to fly and something in me gave me the courage to do so. I knew, as a young girl, I could leave all those things that bind me to Earth and take a leap of faith. That feeling is still with me, helping me fly through all the obstacles that have come my way.

I had a difficult childhood in Peshawar till we moved to Delhi in May 1947. I was one of five siblings and we stayed with our mother and maternal grandfather. My father was a miserable man who knew how to produce children but never had time for them. He ended up in jail and my mother became more desolate than ever. She, a highly educated woman, studied medicine but never took her final exams as instead she got married. In her early life, she was brought up as a princess with a father who was so proud to have her as a daughter. However, as she grew up, she was to lead the life of a wife to this man whom she had to beg for money, almost every single day, for the welfare of her children.

My sister had a similar fate to my mother. She bore seven children and her husband, who was a very simple man, got charged with embezzlement and was put behind bars. She, like my mother, did not have the strength to face life thereafter. It was then that I decided never to marry and lead a life like theirs. I learnt how to read at the age of five and my grandfather gave all his support. It was through my passion for reading books that I found an escape into the parallel life of the characters I read, hence finding happiness that kept me going.

With bad conditions prevailing throughout the country, we were told to pack up and move to India in May 1947. We came to Delhi via Rawalpindi and Haridwar, and made our base in Hanuman Colony. Contrary to popular belief, Partition was a door to heaven for many women of my age at the time. Suddenly times had changed and we had the liberty to take up a vocation and make something of ourselves. Partition was a problem for the rich and the secure. We were not rich and neither had we left any fortune behind. The obstacle that lay in front of me was to earn money so I could get through my education. It was then that I started teaching children as well as working at All India Radio. That became a deterrent too. Wherever I went, my auburn hair seemed to attract attention. No one had ever seen anyone like this before. People started taunting, calling me a 'working girl', suggesting to my mother that I was perhaps involved in activities of ill repute. She threatened to kill herself if I did not stop working but I did not budge. I started covering my head and continued to work. My priority, then, was to have financial independence so that I could prevent myself from suffering the same fate as my mother and sister.

But as they say, destiny has its own plans and the hair that had made so many people jealous also brought love into my life. My husband, Mahendra Kaul, was an ace broadcaster for All India Radio and a very well-known personality. Without any further thought, he gave me a letter proposing to me and I refused. The idea of marriage repelled me and I was in no mental state to say 'yes' to anyone for a lifetime commitment. Around the same time, my brother had fallen for a Christian girl but had vowed to only marry after I got married. My brother's fiancée played foul and found out about the brewing love Mr Kaul had for me, portraying the completely opposite scenario in front of him to make him believe that I yearned for him too. This only served to heighten his courage to approach me again. This time my brother got involved and I couldn't refuse, asking instead for six months to prepare myself for marriage.

We got married on 5 May 1955 and had to leave for Washington DC, USA, as he was called by Voice of America to head the Hindi/International Broadcasting Unit. Within a few days of our landing in the country, Mr Kaul had to lead the launch of the Hindi Broadcasting Unit. However, he came down with jaundice as a result of hepatitis and I had to immediately step up into his shoes and look into the arrangements. Everyone loved my work and within no time I believed my presence was felt. During his tenure at Voice of America as Editor, I helped my husband learn and read Hindi so he could edit scripts comfortably. I was also his punch bag and got the brunt of most of the work that people working under him did, as he could not tell them off directly, instead using me as an outlet for his anger and frustration. At home he was no better – a very difficult man. We saw five years of our married life in Washington where I learnt a lot about both my work and marriage.

Before we got married, Mr Kaul had applied for a job at BBC London. After five years they contacted him with a vacancy. The organisation wanted to start an immigrant programme and he was the best person to fill in as a broadcaster. By then I had finished my Master's in Library Science from Washington DC. In January 1961, we moved to London with our one-month-old daughter, Kalyani, and life changed for us yet again. I took up my first job as a librarian in August to make ends meet. Kalyani was eight months old when I decided to work again and it almost killed me inside to leave her with a part-time nanny. My husband used to be away in Birmingham for five days every week and I was in London, working and nurturing Kalyani. There was not a single day when I did not cry; every day at lunch I would cry my heart out, wipe my tears and wait for the day to be over. Many a time I wanted to leave it all behind and go back to India. Five days of the week were spent at the library and at the weekends I helped out at BBC Studios as someone who would do odd jobs here and there. Back then, the BBC's policy wouldn't allow a husband and wife to work together in the same company, which is why I used to spend my weekends as an informally hired employee. Those days I hardly saw my husband and I feel I may have neglected my family. But this was something that I had to do for us and I somehow gathered all my strength and sailed through it.

In 1968, the BBC launched *Nai Zindagi Naya Jeevan*, which was the first major programme for Hindi- and Urdu-speaking viewers. Each episode would consist of national and international news, a cultural programme and a celebrity interview, presented by Mahendra ji and Saleem Shahed. Most households would wake up early on a Sunday to watch his show from 9am to 10am, and overnight my husband became the most sought-after man in the United Kingdom. Slowly I found myself in the company of the UK's *crème de la crème*, wining and dining with the who's who. My knowledge from being an avid reader coupled with my sense of humour took me a long way with people and I enjoyed their company.

Doors of opportunity opened one after the other. We bought a house, put Kalyani through a good education and ventured into the hospitality industry, starting a restaurant called 'Gaylord' in partnership with our friends from India – a concept still running successfully on Regent Street in London today. Many celebrities have been entertained here and I made it my personal goal to ensure that the entertainment was the best we could offer. From Woody Allen, to The Beatles and Pandit Ravi Shankar to Indira Gandhi and Margaret Thatcher, I saw myself in the company of many such eminent personalities.

In 1977, BBC Radio offered me the chance to take up the position of a full-time producer/broadcaster after my husband moved to BBC TV. Kalyani too had become quite independent and I suddenly saw myself as more settled and adapted to the life I was leading. My daughter was never quite happy with me though. She always felt we neglected her when she needed us the most. All my life I have been a very strong woman who has never shed a tear for herself. However, my only disappointment lies in how I could not help in shaping my daughter's life the way a mother should. Professionally, she has made me proud in every way – she was appointed as the Circuit Judge in 2015. But she couldn't make a home, about which I feel dreadful. Tangled in those orthodox religious beliefs of 'you cannot marry anyone but a Kashmiri Pandit', we kept her away from meeting the man of her dreams. Eventually, she ended up marrying an Irish man, which was the most inapt choice from the beginning. She's now divorced with two children and I cannot help but take this blame on myself.

I have never been a good wife either, never the ideal type. But there is something I must tell you: I have the best joke books in the world. Any time Mahendra ji blew his top, I would shut myself in a room and read these books. A little chuckle, and I was ready for the world again. My journey had to be this way because I chose it to be so and I think I did a relatively fine job by living my struggles joyously. The only advice I can give to all the young people reading this is that whatever is to happen, will happen; it is up to you whether you deal with it merrily or miserably. I find myself very lucky to have found the happiness which even people made of money don't. What else could I have asked for?

I am a healthy eighty-seven-year-old woman and I'd rather die this way than be dependent on anyone. Today as I sit and reflect on the life I have led, my greatest achievement has been my relationships, which I have built over the years. Never have I thought of causing harm or breaking any affiliations (big or small) that I have had with anyone. I have not let anything break – never a crack or a split, not even with my Peshawar. It has been very difficult to physically go back to my city, which taught me how to take fearless flight. But even today, from time to time, I go there in my mind.

Rajni with Pandit Ravi Shankar (wearing white – centre), together with Peter Sellers (left) and Annapurna Devi and George Harrison (right)

Members of the Indian services sing Indian national songs at the Republic Day party at Voice of America

TEN

The Framework of a Woman
SEEMA MALHOTRA MP

Seema Malhotra was elected Labour and Co-operative Member of Parliament for Feltham and Heston in December 2011, and re-elected with an enhanced majority in 2015. From 2014 to 2015, she served as Shadow Home Office Minister for Preventing Violence Against Women and Girls where she led on aspects of the Serious Crime Bill for Labour. Prior to entering Parliament, Seema was a freelance business and public service adviser. She has over ten years' experience with leading firms Accenture and PricewaterhouseCoopers working in strategy and IT systems development. She is the founder and president of the Fabian Women's Network. Seema is on the Fabian Society Executive Committee and a former chair of the Fabian Society.

"Her contemporary approach in politics had me intrigued from the moment we met at a charity event hosted by the British Asian Trust. Her story is one of humble beginnings and one that must be told with compassion."

ANITA GOYAL

I was born in Hammersmith in 1972, into a family of eight. We lived above the family shop – my grandmother from my father's side, my parents, my three older sisters and a younger brother – and looking back as an adult I realise now that we didn't have a lot. I think when you're older, you are afforded the opportunity to look back on your life through the eyes of hindsight, and it is only now that I realise we lived a very local life with really only just enough to make ends meet.

Though I was born in Hammersmith we grew up in Hounslow, so the seat I now represent as an MP relates very much to that area. Growing up, life was challenging for my parents and I do remember my mother in particular somehow managing to cook for a family of eight and care for my grandmother; it seemed as though she was always tired. My grandmother was elderly and our life did revolve around her to an extent. She and I were very close and I believe she was one of my main links with India as a child, as we couldn't afford to visit there often, and I only vaguely recall a trip taken there when I was three or four years old, accompanied by my mother and my younger brother.

My father's family were from an area of India which is now within Pakistan, and my mother's family were from Gojra – again, now in Pakistan. However, both families were forced to move into different parts of India during Partition. My father's family were a little more well off than my mother's, and what I do know about my paternal grandfather is that he died when my father was just a baby. This left my grandmother, my father's mother, a single parent in one of the most difficult times in Pakistan; Father often used to tell us stories of how his mother would feed her children and save nothing for herself, so he would pretend he wasn't hungry so as to share his portion with her. To earn money, she would sew throughout the night, but the pressures on her being a single parent – and not being literate – were huge.

When they came down to India, my father's family settled in Delhi while my mother's family were down in Jalandhar which is an ancient city in the north Indian state of Punjab – and which is where they still reside to this day. I think my father remembers that particular time of his life as extremely difficult, which is one of the reasons why he wanted to leave India. He wanted to give his family a better chance somewhere new. He had a dream initially of becoming a doctor, but the family couldn't afford his studies. Instead he studied engineering and managed to get a scholarship through the Indo-German Institute, which ultimately brought him over to the United Kingdom in 1963.

He qualified as an engineer and in 1965 had an arranged marriage to my mother, who was based in Jalandhar at the time. The marriage was arranged by a mutual friend of both of my grandmothers, and within four weeks of meeting, my parents had married and moved back to the UK. Not long after, my grandmother joined them and they had their first baby – my eldest sister.

My father had brothers but decided that he wanted to take on the responsibility of caring for my grandmother. He was closer to her than his older brothers, and it was decided that life in the UK was the best option for her. I remember her as very present throughout our childhood, and though I recognise the difficulty my mother must have faced in living with her mother-in-law – a typically traditional woman with old-fashioned values around relationships in the home – for us children it was really wonderful to have our grandmother around. Of course, these values are constantly changing these days, and I believe things did change over the course of our lives in terms of power play within the family.

We grew up feeling equally valued and educated, and both of our parents drove us to study hard and succeed in our school work. In that respect I believe they were quite ahead of their time, which was supported by the fact that my mother had studied to postgraduate level back in India and had held off marriage until the age of twenty-six – quite unusual for a young woman in India.

My mother's family are mostly still in India, with only herself and one of her six sisters now based in the UK. My mother's sister is in Ealing now and I visit her as often as I can as we grew up with her and my cousins around all the time and so hers is a relationship I truly value. Diwali was always held at my aunt's house when we were growing up, and I remember to this day the sparklers and fireworks that we would have in the back garden every year, and the trolley that my aunt would bring the feast out on.

When I look back on my life, there are a number of individuals who have influenced my journey and the woman I have become.

My mother, of course, has had a huge impact on who I am today. As we grew up above a shop, she was always around in the day no matter how busy she was, though looking back I don't feel like she always had the time to spend with us. She was physically present, and yet she was never relaxed, always rushing around cooking and looking after everybody. She didn't even eat with us, preferring instead to feed everybody else and eat whatever was left over once the rest of us were finished. Life was always about just getting through the day and making ends meet, and when money was scarce my mother would pick up shift work at friends' shops. Despite all this, and the feeling that we never really spent much time with her, I believe that her sense of steadiness in life was a really big influence; even when things were difficult, it was I who used to argue with my father a lot rather than my mother.

One of the reasons I originally became so interested in politics was seeing how girls and boys are treated so differently. My brother was only two years younger than me, and so I would notice very clearly when things were different. For example, my brother would always get more money than me from the tooth fairy, and he wasn't allowed to do the washing-up, though he eventually rebelled against that rule and in fact became particularly good at washing up. He is a feminist now and argues for the rights of women, motivated probably by the five girls he grew up alongside. When I was eight years old I began to call my father 'SD', short for Sex Discriminator, which I must have picked up from somewhere, and though it sounds silly now, this was an important foundation for me in terms of gender politics and fighting the gender battle we all faced.

I don't think I gave it much thought at the time, but my father had obviously left a lot behind – including his support – and so in challenging situations he must have felt quite alone, surrounded by a family of females including his own mother. Who knows what difficulties or traumas he had faced in his own life. Now we think very differently about friendships and support, and things are somewhat easier, but at the time they were a source of tension. My mother was always very calm and this was a positive influence for me; little would they have ever thought that these experiences would sow the seeds for my own life journey and direction, noticing when things aren't right or equal and initiating the necessary change. In short, I began to learn, and still believe now, that we don't have to live our lives according to decisions that were made years before by somebody that we don't know.

Meanwhile, at school I was a quiet student. I was sociable, but I focused mostly on my studies and felt forever in the shadow of my older sisters. My eldest sister went to Cambridge University and became an engineer, now based in California where she works with racing cars and their engines, testing and building. My second sister went to Newcastle University and became a doctor, while my third sister works in public health in the West Midlands. My brother lives in Australia with a career in computer systems, so we really have spread out across the globe. No one would believe that we all started off above a shop in Osterley.

Much of what we have managed to achieve is due to the sacrifices that have been made by those before us, and while I mention my mother and her dedication to her family in my speeches, I don't really know if she understands how grateful we are.

My father also gave up a lot; when his company relocated to Belgium, he chose to put family stability first and keep us all together. Looking back now as an adult, I recognise that he must have left behind some unfulfilled dreams. He sadly passed away four years ago, and though I think he would have always liked to have had a little more money for himself, in reality he made the choice to be the primary carer for my grandmother and to provide us with a stable home life while we were growing up. He never complained and he always referred to his children as "gifts from God", but I think he always felt the slight hardship. The experience of growing up in India post-Partition stayed with him, and while he had a certain fondness for India, he never had a desire to go back.

One of the stories he used to tell us was of his first arrival in London, expecting a great, grand city, and instead being faced with the reality: cold, grey, and rainy seasons. But my father was a classic economic migrant and he loved Britain. I don't think any of us now can imagine what it must have been like to make the kind of trip that he did, taking a big step into the unknown and leaving his family behind, but he worked hard to make ends meet, with long hours and very basic living. There are people I have come across only recently – a couple – who told me that in the 1960s they rented a room out to my parents, and it was incredible for me to get an insight into my parents before their children came along.

As well as his love of Britain, my father loved cars, and I remember the big American car that we grew up with, with wings at the back. It was a Ford Fairlane – the sort of car that wouldn't look out of place on the set of a movie like *Grease* – and we all used to pile in and sit on each other's lap when we took day trips in the car. Dad loved that.

Another huge influence in my life, both now and back when I was a child, was a particular teacher at school, who taught me English. I think most people have a teacher that inspired them if they really think about it – someone who taught you to see with a new perspective, and think beyond the words on the page. One of our assignments in this particular half term was to go and get worked up about something; I remember I got worked up about Margaret

Thatcher. Looking back, I see now that I was beginning to develop a stronger political awareness. Similarly, in my junior school elections we argued for better pensions for the elderly; I don't remember much beyond the fact that we didn't win, but I do remember that my passion for the argument was inspired by my grandmother who used to collect her meagre pension from the post office. So my teacher and these young experiences influenced me to go to Warwick University and study Politics and Philosophy, and then I got a job as a management consultant.

Earlier in my story I touched on the one trip we made to India when I was a child, aged about three or four. Before I went to university, I had planned to take a year out and visit India, and so at the age of eighteen I went to India for three months on my own – without the express permission of my parents. This might seem strange, but my sisters had paved somewhat of a path of independence for me; by the time it got to me, I don't think my parents were paying too much attention to what I was doing. They didn't necessarily agree with the subjects I chose to study, but it was so important to me to follow my own decision. Even now I believe it is vital to remember that you are the one that has to live with your choices, and so you should always make sure you are living your own dream and not somebody else's.

During my three months in India, the highlight for me was that I got to see so much of my family. It was a true immersion into my past and into my family's life, and it was through my aunt that I picked up a lot of Punjabi; I used to write down words that she said to remind myself later. I visited Delhi and Bangalore, and saw individuals from both my mother's and my father's side of the family, and I truly think the trip changed my identity. I felt that in England I had grown up as part of a minority, and that affected my confidence as a child. But when I was in India, I remember the very different feeling of being part of the majority, and it was a comforting feeling. When I returned to the UK it felt like a culture clash; I brought back with me an Indian accent and wore Indian clothes, and somehow felt much more aware of what it felt like to be the minority. If anything, I think this deepened my understanding of why equality is so important, and why being different is not a bad thing or something to be ashamed of.

By stepping outside your comfort zone, you reduce and tackle the issue of unconscious bias. Behind every front door is a human – with a past, and a story, and a life – and we must learn to break through the barriers between us to accept every fellow human.

My grandmother had passed away when I was thirteen, so my trip to India also gave me a chance to learn about her as she had been; for my thirteen years of life with her, I had only known my grandmother in Britain, out of the context of her own life. Likewise, I feel now as though I only knew my parents as they were with me and not in the context of the life they had grown up in; it's like naming the flower without seeing the plant, and so the India trip really opened my eyes and helped me understand who my parents were as well. As a result of the trip I became closer to the Asian community in Britain, and probably now visit India once or twice a year to keep solid ties to my second home. I am British and yet, additional to my identity as a British woman and a member of the Labour Party, I have Indian heritage, and I am driven by the desire to think about foundations and relationships between people and cultures, as these often form the basis on which prosperity can be built.

My sisters have always been a driving force in my life, and I absolutely have learnt and followed in their footsteps to an extent. My oldest sister was the first to travel by herself, while my second sister always looked after others and instilled a deep family focus that was really important. She set a standard for having a base that you know and are comfortable in, and was a very homely presence. My third sister had an arty side that I vividly remember growing up, and when she learnt to play the guitar I followed in her footsteps and did the same. We were all exploring our own identity in different ways and accepting our cultural heritage alongside our Western surroundings. I am a strong advocate that young people should learn their mother tongue as young as they can; exposure to languages as a young person is such a privilege, and today I am incredibly supportive of communities that have set up organisations to teach language and cultural arts.

Arts and performance are huge passions of mine and I believe they are huge investments not only in children's lives but in our shared futures, because those children will grow up with cultural familiarity and confidence to build strong bridges between nations through things like the arts.

There have been some great influencers in my life, but I have also experienced changes in direction that have had a big impact on my journey. Running for elected office, when I thought I would win but didn't, had a big knock-on effect for me. I had taken a break from my career at Accenture in order to run for office, but I didn't make it and felt really deflated. It felt like such a public knock-back and really taught me to never take anything for granted; I had expected to win but I hadn't, and that was a tough lesson to learn. It shifted my attitude towards elections as well; now I don't take a single voter for granted and believe that every day is a day in which you can achieve something new because tomorrow it may not be there anymore. In fact, I ended up taking on greater responsibility in the local Party rather than in an elected office, teaching me that opportunities are what you decide to make of them. One door closes, but another three may open.

I went on to become Chair of my local Party at the age of twenty-nine. In a position like that people start to look up to you and you are the bridge between the Party and the Member of Parliament, lending you to some of the challenges between the two. I was able to develop my own sense of what needed improving and what could be changed, and we had a really great team with a strong development plan. I think we made a big difference in those three years, and from there I ended up standing for the London Assembly, giving me the chance to experiment with how to campaign for a senior-level office and become noticed by the National Party. I wasn't successful, but the experience sowed the seeds of running a good campaign, learning through trial and error, and building the team up. I developed a strong network of peers and soon became recognised by the Asian community as there weren't many Indian women trying for office like I was. It was the Asian community that had sacrificed, like my parents, to get to where it was, building a base within a local political party; I felt enormous respect for what it was going through. I believe many in that community saw me as a daughter, or a role model for their daughters taking up an active role in the community.

I was mentored by a few female MPs over the years, including Meg Munn MP, who has now stepped down; Barbara Follett MP, wife of Ken Follett; and Barbara Keeley who is still an MP. I think mentors are very important; I had a mentor in Accenture and I learnt that this is someone who you can set goals with, separate to a line manager, and work with to achieve those goals. I went on a very good training course through the Labour Women's Network where we were forced to challenge everything: from how you dressed to the way you looked at the camera; the way your voice sounded on a recording to how to communicate your own brand. In politics we all have our own brand and our own sense of what we're doing, and while you're fighting for your ultimate purpose, you also tackle the issues that are coming to light all the time. I feel that I am constantly delivering on current projects while also working on the ultimate goal of my career.

I believed, and still believe now, that if someone puts a ladder down to help you get up to the next level, it is your responsibility to leave the ladder where it is and help out whoever is waiting below you. One of the major things I did was set up the Fabian Women's Network, which now runs independently with its own elected committee. The driving force behind that was recognising both the importance and power of women's networks, and the importance of connecting women to the processes of power. Familiarity breeds confidence.

I suppose we set up the Women's Network because prior to this there were never really any women on the panels or in the magazines. Now, however, we have six Fabian Women in the cabinet, fifteen ministers in the Labour government and seventy Fabian Women parliamentarians. In my view it wasn't because the women weren't there to do the roles, but because they simply weren't reaching out and putting themselves forward. So, I launched the network in 2005, to breed a network of confident and capable women. Harriet

Harman was one of my first guest speakers and we formed a connection that is still there to this day; I supported her campaign to get elected as Deputy Leader of the Party, and when she was Acting Leader, she asked me to go in and help on some of her gender policy work. So that allowed me to learn a lot about Parliament before I even got elected myself, giving me a confidence and an ability to share my own experience.

Through the Women's Network we then set up the mentoring scheme to educate women in politics. One of the things I had found was that people didn't understand politics as an industry; a truly skilled and professional politician is somebody that can change society or aspects of society, and can jump between local and national issues at the drop of a hat. You have to become comfortable and resilient in stepping up to what that responsibility means; as a politician you must be able to make people feel completely confident in your views through the best possible representation.

I personally am very passionate about visiting schools and community organisations, and so in 2018 I ran our first political education summer school for young people. This gave them the opportunity to learn different behaviours in different environments, and allowed me to share the world I live in that they can play a part in.

I got married to my husband in 2005, and he has been a huge support to me. He is probably a hundred times more intelligent than anyone else I know, and yet he has a humble demeanour about him that gives him a perspective that has proved invaluable to me. He is a senior in his profession, and so his views are important both as a friend but also as a mentor. Our lives are very different and because of that we are mutually supportive of each other. My mother-in-law lives with us and I am so lucky that she seems to embody my husband's support whenever he is away. She comes to a lot of events with me, and we seem to treat each other's lives as equally as important which is amazing. We have been on a journey together as a family and that journey is continuing and developing every day.

Keeping a focus on who I am has always been a vital part of my journey, and I have always given huge importance to giving back. I give money to support charities and good causes where I can, and when I haven't been earning, I have donated my time. There are others in the world and society is important; what we give each other makes the world a safer and better place, and so we must not take anything for granted. I would love to see the Fabian Women's Network go international and I dream of opening a women's political academy. I see it as my responsibility to continue to deliver what I have dedicated my life to, and so I am constantly inspired to drive these dreams forward for women everywhere.

ELEVEN

Always 'Our Daughter'
KALBIR BAINS

I saw Kalbir Bains receive an Asian Women of Achievement Award in 2018 for her social and humanitarian work, and somehow I knew she would lend me her story for all of us to read. She is an author; a modern visionary, who knows that a definite change needs to be brought about – change in lifestyle, change in actions and in the mind. She is one of us, yet it is her sense of being vocal that sets her apart. To sum up what she has gone through in a few words would not be enough. She is a survivor, self-made woman and the author of *Not Our Daughter! The True Story of a Daughter-in-Law*.

AASTHA K SINGHANIA

What I thought was a normal upbringing, wasn't. It was when I stepped into university that I realised pretending to have both parents on your side wasn't a thing in this century. All through our growing years, we've always maintained a double life, where my mother and father were virtually present even though they divorced many years ago. Divorce was a word that our family had never heard of. However, it was repeated twice: once with my mum and once with me.

My maternal grandmother was born in Pakistan (undivided India). Her approach to life and living was way beyond her years. Although she had to bow down to the cruel conditions of Partition and forced all her daughters to get married at the earliest age she could, she made sure all of them were educated, which was a rarity in itself at the time. My mother too was put on a plane to come to London, where her sister had seen this boy who they thought was the perfect match for her. She got married in 1979 and realised he was somebody she did not know at all, somebody she did not know even when they parted ways.

Within their first year of marriage, they had us – my twin sister and me. My grandmother couldn't fathom the idea of the family's firstborn as girls and gave my mother a hard time. One day my father decided that enough is enough and moved out of her house, about twenty houses down the road. Within two years, they had another girl and not one person came to visit my mother in the hospital, except for her sister and my father's sister. However, when my brother came along, the whole family was there to celebrate the 'birth of a boy' in the house. Even us sisters didn't get to see him for three full days. My mother, who always complained about not being given any respect in the house, was suddenly put on a pedestal. The celebration went on for a year, till we celebrated his first birthday with pomp and gusto. That evening, my father drank the night away and we realised that his old habit of drinking had come back.

My father was addicted to alcohol and gambling before he got married. A few years into the marriage, it came back and had a knock-on effect on our lives. He started to miss work, so there was no household income, which led to the banks knocking at our door to chase the mortgage payments. He used to beat my mother a lot too. She had to take up odd jobs to step into the role of father, so she could avoid asking him for money. It was at that time she realised how ironic her life was compared to what my grandmother had envisaged for her. Sometimes, we get attracted to the glitter of a place, thinking that our children will have a better life getting out of India. My nani (maternal grandmother) probably thought the same for my mother. But she felt more hardship bringing us all up – going out to work, looking after the house and the children and still being able to find time to see relatives and worry about our father. In India, it is easy to divide the work amongst people in the house, but for her, her only saviours were my twin sister and myself. One evening, my father had mixed his dose of antibiotics and alcohol and lost all bearing of what he was doing and where he was. He beat my mother black and blue. I remember all four children were trying to get him to stop but he continued to punch her. He went straight for her neck, snatched at her gold chain and paused for ten seconds. My mother bolted for the door and ran to the neighbours. The police came, the social services got involved and he was put into a cell. No one from the family came to see my mother, no one acknowledged us. Even today my mother lives twenty houses down the road from my grandfather but no one has ever come to say hello.

There comes a point in a woman's life when she realises that she can't bear any more agony. That was my mother's breaking point and she decided to step away from her marriage. My nani called her from India and kept telling her, "divorce *na kari*" (whatever you do, do not divorce him). There was a lot she had to go through, there was a lot of pressure: pressure of what people are going to think, pressure of how a divorce is unacceptable in society, pressure of the unsaid trouble of getting the three girls married and how she would run the house. But she bravely put everything behind her and got ready to face the rest of her life.

Her first aim in life was to get my sister and me married, only because my brother had a girlfriend at the time and she would rather have the girls settled down first before the boy of the house. We, particularly I, were the least interested in marriage. I had to go through bypass surgery a few years ago, which impacted the blood circulation on the left side of my body. I lost movement and was bedridden for almost a year. I was dating somebody at the time but he called the relationship off as soon as I fell ill and that took away all my confidence and faith in falling in love again. I recovered and decided to give up meat and alcohol and made the gym the most visited place in my life. I ran the London Marathon in 2012 and slowly got myself involved with work. I was a fashion designer, working in Oxford, and had a lovely social life. My mother was still very keen for me to find the right person to spend my life with and my friend got me on the Southall wedding list. I met many men: some wanted me to leave my career for them, some wanted to change my style of dress and others wanted me to come home at a particular time. No one was worth a second meeting. It was only later when I had taken a back seat that a family kept ringing our house so their son could meet me. It came out later that the boy had seen me at a wedding and was hounding his parents to take the next step forward. We got talking and realised we had a lot in common and he proposed marriage to me within three months.

Within two months of my marriage I fell pregnant. My mother had clocked this well before I knew it, owing to my ratty behaviour. I told my husband and he immediately reminded me of our five-year plan of having a house, excelling in our careers etc, and stated that we were not having this baby. I cried to my best friend who suggested I try talking to him one more time but he refused outright and told me to sort out the 'mess' alone. Unfortunately, he didn't realise that it takes two to get into this mess but it was on me to sort this out by myself. It was at this time that I had a reality check and noticed the similarity between my life and my mother's. Whenever there was a family function, she refrained from taking my father with us due to his drink problem and always lied to everyone who asked after him, saying that he was at work. And here I was, in a big family house, lovely in-laws, newly married and keeping up this pretence that everything was well in my life too, while in reality I was leading a double life just like my parents did.

It was my birthday two days after I had found out about my pregnancy and my in-laws had invited my entire family for celebrations. I was nauseous and felt sick the entire time and was going through this strange anxiety where I wanted to share the turmoil with my family and speak to someone – but I wasn't allowed to mention my pregnancy to anyone. I heard my nani speaking to my mother and thanking the Lord for blessing the present generation with lovely spouses, unlike theirs who immersed their lives in the high of alcohol. The irony of the situation was that alcohol is not the only problem in a marriage and I knew that everything would go downhill from here.

I terminated my pregnancy the following week and caught an infection. This led to depression and my behaviour at home was being questioned because no one had any clue about it. My husband and I stopped sleeping in the same bed, even though we appeared to be this happy and 'in love' couple to the rest of the world. On the work front, my design manager told me not to terminate the pregnancy because they were not going to extend my contract, and so I faced my only happy place also being taken away from me. My husband became aggressive towards me and a couple of times hit the door, only just missing my face. My mother-in-law questioned me about what I had done to make him so angry, while my father-in-law casually walked out to get the door repaired. I noticed that there was no acknowledgement of his behaviour at home and hence began to understand the extent of gender inequality that exists for women even after marriage. A woman is supposed to leave her parents, her career, her life for a new family who she accepts with all her heart but in return does not get the respect she is due, which shows how unjust our society can be sometimes. I loved dancing and was trained to be a *kathak* (Indian form of dancing) dancer but couldn't take it up because my in-laws thought society would not accept a daughter-in-law dancing away, not understanding that *kathak* is an art form which is not supposed to be looked down upon.

Sometimes, a woman can be her own worst enemy. As a daughter-in-law to the generation before, which was definitely a harder time to live in, my mother-in-law should have been more tolerant of the changing times and modernity setting in. If her in-laws did not allow her to do certain things in the

1950s, why must the same rules be levied for me in the twenty-first century? Times change and so do people; I wish people had a better understanding of what it takes to let a human being live in peace. Even after a year of marriage things did not settle down. We kept arguing and I started to discover things I did not know about. I was never given a set of house keys and that meant always asking for permission to enter my own house. I wasn't allowed to go anywhere myself, so was dropped at the station and picked up. One day I came home earlier and had to justify to my father-in-law why I didn't call him to pick me up. I wasn't even allowed on business trips by myself and when I fought my way out of that, I had to call the family every evening so that they could make sure I was back in my room by 7pm. The last nail in the coffin was when I found out that the house phone lines had been tapped and were recording every outgoing and incoming conversation in a little box in my in-laws' room. I felt a sense of betrayal, that I was kept in darkness for so long and did not know anything about this boy and his family, despite dating him for some time before getting married. I realised there was a difference in lifestyle and upbringing. My mother had made sure that we were financially independent, something she learnt was important from her own experiences. This, however, was not given any importance in his family and I saw that my husband was a mollycoddled child owing to the fact that he was the only son in the family. It was a different setup, something I couldn't get used to. And the day they thought I was going to confide in my family about all of this, they changed the locks of the house. That was the end of everything. I packed a small bag and left for good.

Since then my question to society has been: Till when will we women see the oppression of people around us in so many different forms? During my wedding, there was a clear demarcation of *ladkewale* and *ladkiwali*, which was not needed. During the reception, my mother and my family pitched in to pay the expenses of hosting 500 people. I had to step in and ask my in-laws to bear the expenses of the party. The rest of it, down to the first festival in my married year, was taken care of by my grandmother, mother, uncles and me. But, for what? My marriage did not even last two years. I decided to write my book and create awareness within the Indian community, all over the world, that instead of wasting money on entertaining people only because this is the norm these days, give that money to the couple to start a happy married life. In polite language we call this *lena-dena*, but it is actually dowry abuse.

My family was not happy when I wrote my book and my aunt asked me why I had decided to wash my dirty laundry in public. But I know that if I hadn't given my example, there was no other way to initiate the change I want to bring about in this world. I have teamed up with a group of girls in Birmingham, who, along with their headmistress, will allow me to put my book up for AQA GCSE coursework. After my abortion, I decided to work on the shame and stigma attached to the laws of abortion. My husband asked me to go to an abortion clinic outside Milton Keynes so that no one knew what we were going through. How many girls have been in the position of losing a child and going through the trauma by themselves? I had my family stand by me and help me out of this situation. Not many have the same structure; rather they push girls back to lead their lives the way they have been doing so that their family name is not tarnished. I decided to set up an education system for safeguarding these laws and help these girls realise that it is okay to take a stand for their own self. I am of course proud that my work has been so widely recognised, but this is in no way the motivation for my passion. I have received recognition in a *Glamour* magazine article on International Women's Day 2018 and from the Sikh Network Team who both noted me as an inspirational role model. While the titles and awards don't matter, the idea of being a role model pushes me forward even on the most difficult days, as I know that what I stand for is important.

We have to be the change within. A dialogue, which leads to a discussion, helps bring about change. It is when we speak of our miseries that the other person gets the courage to face their own. I urge this generation to stand up for yourself and don't let anyone or anything undermine you. I remember when I was going through my separation and my father got to know about it, he said sadly, "I can't believe you had to go through all of this by yourself." I looked at him and pointed out the time when he did that to his own wife, the woman who bore his children, the woman who loved him and the woman he was supposed to spend the rest of his life with. Suffice to say his realisation dawned on him and I think that was when I realised I had taken my first step towards #change.

*Kalbir's mother with a friend, at her friend's
wedding in Gunachau, Punjab, in 1972*

*Kalbir's parents' wedding day, 29 May 1979,
near Birmingham in the West Midlands, UK*

TWELVE
Unknown Land, Unknown Life
MANI K BAJWA

On a cold snowy Tuesday afternoon, I set out to meet Ms Bajwa at her house in London. Unlike my other interviewees, I did not know much about her. As I made my way to the meeting, in my mind I was trying to pencil down the questions I would ask. When I reached her place, I was welcomed into a beautiful home, dressed in pictures of her young self and her children. The wooden floor matched well with the beige tapestry and the white snow, which fell silently in the background, adding to the warmth the place radiated. You could hear a soft, serene tune playing in the background, which screamed of the story she had for me. The beautiful setup and the positivity in the room calmed my fears and I knew where to begin.

AASTHA K SINGHANIA

Every time I woke up and opened the curtains of my bedroom window, I could see the vast green fields with endless yellow mustard flowers – *sarson ke khet* as we call them; a view which would bring a smile to my face. It was nice to start my day with the sun beaming onto my face, breathing in *meri mitti ki khushboo* (fragrance of the soil). You could always hear someone somewhere in the house either bickering over something trivial or laughing at the breakfast table. I was used to waking up to this hustle bustle, in a world which we had made for ourselves, in the middle of nowhere – a place where I was never left alone.

I was born on 25 February 1965 in District Patiala, Punjab, India, to a massive Punjabi Jatt household where my father was a noted politician. Being the youngest of four siblings, I was the most pampered by everyone in the house. Everything was looked after and I didn't have to lift a finger. My father was of a very liberal mindset and never questioned my dreams or prevented us from doing what we wanted to. He made sure we went to the best schools and nurtured a 'go-getter' personality. I wanted to become a politician myself and at the age of fifteen, I started with my graduation in Economics and Social Science from Chandigarh, Punjab. My family cared and had opened all doors to let us fly in the direction we wanted to go. But however cosmopolitan they were in other matters, they did not give me a choice in making the most important decision of my life.

By the end of my second year of university, my parents had found a boy who I was to marry and move to the United Kingdom with. I did not know who he was or what he did and within three months I found myself in Scunthorpe, a town in northern England. Reality set in and at the age of seventeen I had to suddenly take on the role of a married, responsible woman. At that age, it is difficult for a girl so young to have the knowledge and sense of maturity to tackle a situation like this, and it came as a challenge. I had to massively downsize in terms of culture and community. I, who knew how to blend in with people within minutes, felt out of place in my new surroundings amongst new people, new family and a man I did not know much about at all.

Life was slow and I was unhappy. I used to love being around people, and adjusting in Scunthorpe was becoming tougher. I was never made to feel at home, which led to difficulties between my in-laws and me. Every time I looked to my husband for support, I didn't receive any. Within a few months, I realised that we were very different people on different wavelengths and with different ideas, and this life that I had embraced unknowingly was not going to be easy. He was born and brought up in the UK and therefore his way of living and socialising was far different from mine. The love and the family setup I came from was such a contrast to what I married into. The love I grew up with carved me into a zestful person who had so much love to give. But somehow, this love was never reciprocated from his side and that widened the lack of understanding we had. Within six months of being married, my husband and I moved to London to start our own business. I was elated and thought this would be an opportunity to start again and breathe life into our relationship. However, he and I came from different worlds and it seemed to take a lot to even arrive at a common starting block. Even with our group of friends, we were never on the same page, for I was looking for people who had my dialect and came from my country – someone who I could freely speak to.

Gradually our socialising reduced and I don't remember when I turned so inside out that I became tight-lipped.

Within two years of our marriage I had my daughter, Deep. My son, Manraj, came along after another five years. They became my world and that gave me the strength to continue and live for them. At the time, I was working and looking after our business together with my husband. It was difficult striking a work-home balance with small children. Every morning, like a machine, I would switch on to get started with my day. At a very young age I had to forget myself and dedicate all of me to the children and the family. Women have the power to take on so much at any age, in any role. In any dire situation, we somehow find the strength to fight it and carry on, for we believe in swimming through rather than sinking in. By then, I had changed a lot and started burying every tear and pain in my heart. For the first five years I kept no connection with my family back in India. There was so much emotion pent up inside of me that I feared seeing them would unleash all my anguish and misery, which could have a disastrous effect on the life I had made for myself. My only aim, then, was to get my children settled, happy and prosperous; and I was not prepared to jeopardise this in any way.

I was dying inside and it took me ten years to build something of the relationship I was trying to make with my husband. But by then, it was too late. We had started moving on two different paths, marked by different purposes, which led to two different destinations. Up until that time, I had successfully managed to camouflage our reality and build a façade of happiness for people to see. Everyone envied the 'perfect' life I was leading, but no one knew what I was going through. And then came a time when my depression started to show. People noticed and any time I was questioned about it, tears would stream down my face. Yet I did not utter a single word for there was no way I could have broken down.

Living my life like this for so many years, I think I tested God's patience to the utmost. In 2001, owing to my mental health, I was involved in a major car accident, which left me bedridden for almost six years. It was perhaps God's way of telling me to slow down and to dust off the stubbornness I was living with. My back had suffered terribly and I was forced to pause and reflect on what I was going to do. All this time, I had not paid attention to my emotional needs, which quickly accelerated into depression. In retrospect, those six years were a blessing. It gave me time to hit the brakes on my fast-spiralling life to understand what had gone wrong. I had survived death and I promised myself I would make my second life worth all the pain I went through. Thereon, I vowed to breathe into this precious life the happiness I deserved, by spreading love to people who needed it more.

My depression became an obstacle in my healing process. My doctor suggested I see a psychiatrist who would channel my thoughts in the right way. But as any human would think, I asked myself, am I really mad? Why do I need a psychiatrist? A lot of research and reading up on the subject allowed me to gather the courage to meet and talk to someone, to off-load the weight I'd been carrying on my chest for so many years. This is exactly what I needed; the regular sessions of emotional counselling coupled with physiotherapy got me up and about again by 2010. The first thing I did when I independently took my first step was to set up my charity, Billion Women.

Billion Women champions the rights of women by empowering them and helping them find a voice. Though the organisation's main work is to help and support homeless women, with my workshops I also help in providing strength and solutions to those who have been mentally and emotionally distressed. I wanted to be of help, delivering to others something I couldn't get when I most needed it. I knew the best way I could help was by being a good listener. As simple a thing as talking to someone can help those in difficulty find some stability. When we keep our problems to ourselves, we make them much bigger than they are. Share them. Set free the negative emotions harbouring in you. The minute you do that, those negative thoughts are released into the universe, which then sends you your answer. Sometimes, one needs a lot of strength to say 'no' or to come out of a traumatic relationship. Back then, the way we were brought up, leaving everything and going back was not an option. In fact, we were categorically told that our husband and his house is where we are to be. We were to fight and deal with it, the process of which has seen so many women sacrifice their lives and live unhappily. In that regard, I like this generation, as they don't believe in suffering for the sake of society or pleasing their family. Why shouldn't one stand up and give oneself a chance to be happy and find love once again?

I am a proud woman, for many reasons. I am proud to be doing selfless work for this amazing cause through my organisation. I am proud to have learnt and lived without regrets and pain. I am proud to have made my children what I had dreamt for them – strong individuals capable of getting their voice heard. I am a proud grandmother to two beautiful children from my daughter and son-in-law. I am proud that I have the freedom to choose, to love and to give time to myself.

My greatest achievement is sitting in front of you, talking about my life and spreading positivity. To this day, I have not been able to connect with my husband's family and, six years back, I gave up trying too. Today I have no regrets. However, I feel sorry for the girl who, every morning in Punjab, would look forward to running across the fields to chase after the train that went past her house; whose voice was the loudest and could light up every corner of her house; who had to come to an unknown land with dreams of a new life that every girl harbours; who had to shut away her true self to open doors for who she had become. I send her all my love and am pleased with what she has made of herself.

It wasn't pleasant to share home and work space, on a daily basis, with a person who I never came to know or understand. Eventually, the sentiments between two people start dying but I wanted to keep the love I was filled with alive for my children, so that they are raised in the same loving and happy place that I grew up in.

Mani showcasing her charity Billion Women with Sadiq Khan

Mani discussing her charity endeavours on the radio

Mani with girls in India

THIRTEEN

Creative Vision
MANDEEP RAI

Mandeep's career in journalism spans twenty years, covering print, radio, TV and online, primarily for the BBC and Reuters. Her passion to make a difference, a thirst for knowledge, and a love of people has propelled her to all corners of the globe, travelling to over 140 countries. International development became a source of much of her reporting, working for organisations such as the United Nations, European Commission, and a number of grassroots organisations.

She was awarded a First Women Award for Media in recognition of breaking ceilings in all forms of media. Mandeep is currently working with the CEO of Creative Visions, Kathy Eldon, an organisation that uses the power of media and the arts to ignite positive social change.

"Mandeep (BEcon, MA, MSc, MBA) is a role model for women around the world for her ambition, determination, and vision for the next generation".

ANITA GOYAL

My story begins in Chak 94, a district near Lahore in modern day Pakistan, and the original home of my maternal grandmother Mohinder Kaur. During the Partition of India, she and her family were forced to cross the border to India, alongside thousands of other families, leaving almost everything they had built behind. They were open and extremely community-centred people, with strong Muslim and Hindu friendships. Partition in many ways tore apart their heart, as well as much of their Sikh homeland. Punjab is the birthplace of Sikhi, and it is now split into east and west Punjab, approximately half in Indian and half in Pakistan. The same Punjabi culture still runs through the divided state and its people.

A large proportion of Sikh heritage was left behind in Pakistan, such as the birthplace of the founder Guru Nanak Dev Ji, over 600 gurdwaras, the holy site of the Martyrdom of Guru Arjan Dev Ji, and the sites of massacres which are recited in the Ardas (the Sikh prayer that completes every service). Sadly, there are only thirteen gurdwaras left in Pakistan at present. The massacres site quoted in the Ardas is potentially being sold off in Lahore to create a shopping mall.

When visiting my grandmother's village in Pakistan earlier this year, I saw how everything she spoke about had been destroyed. This was the extent of the loss and tragedy on both sides of the border. Perhaps this is why migration thereafter seemed like the most logical and preferable choice. My grandmother's family eventually settled in the town of Banga, near Ludhiana on the Indian side of Punjab. Over time some of the family migrated to different parts of the world, returning often to contribute to the community through the building of schools, parks, (Baba Gola) and hospitals (Guru Arjan Dev Ji).

My Bibi Ji moved to the US with her family thanks to her brother, Mohan Singh, who sponsored her. Her husband, and my Nana Ji – Harbhajan Singh, and three of her children (under the age of sixteen – Poora – Kamaldeep, Sukhjeevan and Gurtej) were eligible to migrate as dependents. However, my mother, Gurpal Kaur – the eldest of her four children – was seventeen at that time and so there was a question over what would happen to her.

My paternal grandfather, Naranjan Singh (Baba Ji), was already in the UK, part of the wave of migration after the Second World War. While his heart lay in the rich and fertile lands of Punjab, he gave much of his working life to England, following the core ethos of Sikhs: hard work, sacrifice and contribution. It was on a family visit back to Punjab that his youngest son, Resham Singh, spotted my mother at the age of seventeen riding through the village on a bicycle. "I would love to marry a girl like her!" he said. His wish was soon granted. Circumstances colluded, with my mother's family having to leave for the US without her and a proposal for marriage from a family with a strong background. They were agreed to be married during that very trip to India. It seemed like the perfect arrangement for all, except for my mother, for whom it meant sacrificing ambitions of becoming a doctor, in order to move to grey and cold England.

Once in the UK, my mother joined my father's whole family on Regents Street, Smethwick in Birmingham, including my father's three older brothers, Gurdial, Malkit, and Amrik Singh and their wives. My mother worked hard, along with her sisters-in-law Charn, Gurmeet and Simran Kaur. And I see the values of devotion, hard-work and service still in earnest today in them all. They did all this for their future children, and we have striven to make sure we take on those values and stand to make a positive contribution ourselves.

The journey of Sikhs at this time comes amidst the backdrop of Maharaja Ranjit and Daleep Singh's story, which coincided with the end of the Sikh Kingdom in India. Generations of Sikhs who wish to contribute to society in the best possible way thus followed, wherever they were. They may not all necessarily be in Punjab but their values are strong and driven towards seva (service). The Punjabi diaspora around the world, and back in Punjab, dance with all their might, work with all their might and love with all their might.

Among the Sikh community, it is not just a story about the strength of women, but about raising the next generation of the Sikh Kingdom – the story of Maharaja Duleep Singh brought forward to the modern day. So that is what my parents did, they concentrated on giving us all that they could, and they decided to move out of Birmingham to buy a business. They found a shop between Birmingham and Swindon (where my grandmother's sisters Nani Surinder and Nana Dilbag, and Nani Narinder and Nana Pala had shops), in Gloucestershire.

When I was seven years old, and my sister Rajdeep was four, my parents moved to a small village called Churchdown, between Gloucester and Cheltenham, to run a small grocery shop in a council estate. We were the only ethnic minorities in the area and became subject to extreme racism. We had to erect metal bars on the outside of the property after receiving repeated attacks by yobs throwing bricks through the window, one of which hit my mother in the head. Later, windows now covered, a petrol bomb was thrown through the letterbox. One day, on my way to school, a boy was so curious about what colour my blood was (brown or red?) that he decided to trip me up such that I smashed my nose and bled from the fall.

Integrating into life in the UK was a struggle for many Sikhs. Many Sikh men – with traditional uncut hair and turbans – cut their hair in order to integrate into society and improve their chances of finding work. Yet today, in many ways, some Sikhs are turning full circle. My brother, Manreshpal, decided he was the generation that had a choice to embrace his faith. At the tender age of seven, he decided to grow his hair and start to wear a turban. My own children, two boys, are the only Punjabis in their respective central London schools, the only Sikhs, and certainly the only boys with uncut hair (they both wear a patka, a Sikh head covering which is worn by boys before graduating onto full it's 'bigger brother' the turban).

The language, faith, and values have been passed down by the women in my family, who always spoke to us in Punjabi, prayed in Gurmuki and danced to bhangra. Still, it wasn't until my mother sent me to India for the first time, with my granduncle Nana Dilbag and his son Harren, that I saw Punjabi culture and the Sikh faith first-hand. We didn't even have a gurdwara in Gloucester, and so I knew more about Buddhism up until that point than Sikhi. Aged 14, being in Punjab for the very first time, my heart soared. It was like discovering my roots and wings at the same time!

It wasn't always easy, because in India it was clear to the local people that I wasn't 'Indian', and they could tell by the way I would walk or even move my head. Whilst in England I was identified as being Indian. People say that British Indians fall into the gap between two cultures, yet actually we are in the unique position to build a bridge between them and extract the best from both. For this reason, I wanted to better understand what it is to be Punjabi, to know where I had come from and how Punjab had evolved, and more broadly I wanted to know India. And this is exactly what I went on to do years later, when I chose to immerse myself in India for my first year-long assignment as a broadcast journalist.

During that year, I travelled the breadth and depth of India, especially Punjab. I spent time learning gurmuki, ghatka and giddha in Baru Sahib and at the Miri Piri Academy. I lived for a month at Harmandir Sahib, more commonly known as the Golden Temple in Amritsar. It was a rite of passage that helped me understand more about my own faith and more broadly the power of faith in people's lives. Sitting by the sarovar, the sacred pool that surrounds the temple, one could see pilgrims who had travelled huge distances come to bathe in the holy waters for healing and cleansing, and then stand in supplication with utter faith. People came from all over to share their most heartfelt problems, fears, hopes and joy. Seeing day after day how people found strength in faith showed me its power.

In India, faith assumes many avatars: almost all the faiths and religions of the world are represented in a significant way and many were birthed in the original India, including Hinduism, Buddhism, Jainism, and Sikhi. It is obvious that they are believers, for no one in their right mind would get behind the wheel of a car there otherwise, and car windscreens are often decorated with deities. Faith was a clear value for India – and I began to think about what my values were.

Upon reflection my own values hit me hard at the age of eighteen. Being the eldest, I had to fight several pre-defined notions that my family lived by while growing up. For example, when I was interviewed by the Oxford University, unlike many parents who would have expressed support or encouragement, my mother was completely against the idea. To her, a name like Oxford epitomised the English ruling class – those who had changed her native India so much during the Raj, and were ultimately responsible for her ending up in a place where she was alienated, alone, and the frequent victim of violent racial abuse.

She envisioned losing me, her best and only friend where we lived, to a place where I would become reliant on drugs, and end up marrying an upper-class boy probably called Sebastian! The moment the word Oxford passed my lips, my mother was immediately and implacably on the warpath.

"Who will want to marry you if you go there?" were her exact words.

Marriage. At eighteen, it felt like a cage to be avoided for as long as possible. The end of freedom and happiness. Then, as now, what I valued most was the power to set the course of my own life, not to be constrained by the expectations or ambitions of others. For my mother, nothing was more important than to get me married off at the right time and to the right kind of boy. A Sikh, preferably from Punjab, with the appropriate creed, background and parentage.

What both of us feared most was what the other desperately wanted. It was the first time in my life when I really understood the importance of values. For my mother, family and heritage held sway. I, on the other hand, was moved by the desire for freedom, exploration and had a thirst for knowledge.

We both wanted the best for me, but we couldn't agree on what that was. Our starting points and assumptions were too far apart. Our values were in conflict.

In order to appease my idol, best friend and mother, I accepted a place at Manchester University to study Politics, Philosophy and Economics (PPE). In my second year an opportunity arose that put me on yet another collision course with my mother. It was during the Asian Financial Crisis in 1997–98. I had the chance to go to Melbourne and study PPE first-hand, with the supervising experts at the time. Knowing what response I could expect, I didn't share this news with my family until my scholarship was secured, a ticket booked and my flight to Australia just twenty-four hours away.

I finally made the call to let my mother know. Insults were screamed down the phone, Punjabi-style, but the die was cast. I was fortunate that my Mohinder Nani Ji was visiting from the United States, and interceded on my behalf. "It is already written which tap she will drink from – there is nothing we can do or say," were her words. My trip went ahead, on the agreement that no one else – not even my father or siblings – was to know I had left the country.

My journey to study at the University of Melbourne was life changing, and I travelled across South East Asia to get back home – seizing the opportunity to see more of the world and quench my thirst for knowledge first-hand. Only, as my mother had predicted, this thirst was insatiable.

In the last 20 years I have travelled to over 140 countries, reporting as a journalist. In my career the thirst has taken me across finance, international development and media: from working at JP Morgan as a graduate, to travelling the world as a broadcast journalist for the BBC World Service.

I set up the UAE's first media-focused venture capital fund for twofour54, and spent time working within both the UN and EU. I have gained an MSc in Development Economics from the LSE and completed an MBA from London Business School including study at Harvard Business School and MIT.

These varied experiences have given me the opportunity to see how values shape everything from personal and family relationships to local communities and multi-national organisations. As a teenager I had started to understand how values define us as people, framing the direction we choose for our lives. My career has shown me that values are also about how change is achieved and a better world created.

During my first job, at JP Morgan, I gained some insight into the power of values to drive change, working on the early efforts of what is now known as impact investing – backing companies that deliver a social and environmental good, as well as a financial return. Now a widely embraced idea, twenty years ago it was mostly scoffed at by experienced investment bankers.

But it was one of the early signs of a business world moving beyond the 'profit at all costs' mentality towards today's more purpose-driven environment. I would pick up that work some years later, as part of the group with Dean Nitin Nohria at Harvard Business School that developed the Global Business Oath – a response to the global financial crisis which outlined how executives could use values to prevent the same thing from ever happening again.

My MBA, and the experience I gained establishing a media venture capital fund for the Middle East and North Africa (MENA) from Abu Dhabi, helped show me the importance of business values, and how they can be taken from written vision to be put into action.

If my experience in the corporate world gave me one lens on the power of values, an even more powerful one emerged from my years as a journalist. This career change was one that arrived almost completely by accident.

I was at the airport in Cancun, getting ready to visit Cuba for the first time. I had been told that there were two ways to do this. Option 1, join the dollar economy, visiting as a tourist and being treated accordingly; or Option 2, discard any branded items, stay away from hotels and live as a local in the peso economy. With brown skin, curly hair and fluent Spanish, I could just about pass for a Cuban, and was determined to experience Cuba as a Cuban. Option 2. To make this happen however, I found myself in the unusual situation of trying to lose my luggage, with all its giveaway foreigner's clothing, at the airport. Perhaps the strangeness of my needs drew me to the most striking person I could see: a tall woman with flaming red hair dressed in a bright sea green silk suit. I came to know her as Kathy Eldon, a filmmaker with an extraordinary story, who would change my life forever.

Kathy had lived a life of adventure – moving from her native US to England, and then to Kenya with her young family in the 1970s – but one that became clouded in tragedy when her son, Dan, a photojournalist, was stoned to death while working in Somalia in 1993. She went on to build a foundation in his memory, Creative Visions, which supports journalists around the world who are using the media to campaign and achieve positive social change.

By some miracle, and despite the protests of her then pilot boyfriend, Kathy somehow agreed to take my luggage on her flight to LA (to then be left on the carousel so I could later retrieve them from lost property). This was before 9/11 changed attitudes to airport security forever, but even so, it was still decidedly dubious to approach a complete stranger boarding a flight to ask if they would check in your bags.

A few days later I received an email from her which went something like this: "There were sniffer dogs all over your bags as they emerged on the conveyor belt in LA! LAPD Blue had my name on a card, and I am writing to you from a bare prison cell – this is my one consented communication." My mouth ran dry as I scrolled down… "Only joking with ya! In all seriousness, you have the same chutzpah as my son! What are you doing after Cuba? First stop, if you want your bags back – come to my home and get them."

So, one chance meeting turned into another (at her stunning home in LA). We hit it off straight away, and subsequently Kathy made me a job offer. I accepted with delight, ready to immerse myself in the colourful world of LA, the home of Hollywood. Celebrities were in and out of Kathy's home whenever I went to collect my bags. Sting would be on the phone with Kathy, I would bump into Whoopi Goldberg on my way out of the house, and I even let Mariah Carey jump ahead of me in the queue for the bathroom later that evening at a party!

Working with Kathy Eldon created two lasting legacies in my life: firstly, my work with Creative Visions, which continues today. Secondly, a pathway into what has been the most important part of my working life, as a broadcast journalist, reporting on international development and social impact stories from all over the world.

Over almost two decades, my microphone has taken me around the world. My reporting has brought me to the sharp end of some of the inequality and social injustice I had started to grapple with during my time in investment banking. Living in India for a year, I became deeply involved with several grassroots NGOs and covered stories about the extraordinary inequality, and the socio-economic barriers facing women – from unequal rights, to unnecessary widespread illness against women, even in villages where the gender balance of leadership was equal.

Whilst I was reporting from India, a law had been passed asking for fifty percent of all village leadership to be female. I thought this was an excellent initiative until I began to realise that many of the women couldn't perform in that role because they would fall ill every month. Not directly due to their menstruation cycle, but because sanitary pads would be dried in the cow shed to save embarrassment, where disease and illness would easily spread. Tragically, the women themselves were too embarrassed to share what was really going on and it took a lot of time and trust for things to improve. I knew that any of these women could have been me, and I could have been them.

As my reporting experience grew, I was increasingly inspired by the values I saw, and how they were being used by individuals and communities to create change. With my NGO experience and placements with the EU and UN, I had seen how third parties sought to address the social problems I reported on. But the most meaningful change was being driven from the grassroots themselves, by activists who faced no bureaucracy or funding traps.

I believe it is no accident that the power for change is so much greater from the bottom up than top down, and that is because all these campaigns for change are rooted in essential values. The people who are most effective in fighting for progress are those who are doing something for no other reason than they believe in it, and want desperately to make it happen.

It isn't their job, or their requirement as a state organisation, or something their donors compel them to do. It is simply that it matters most to them. It's their mission, one that arises from their values. Equally, the inspiration for change can come from the top, but it only really works when the desire, motivation and need for change is truly felt – not if it is being prescribed.

I have covered numerous stories like this, seeing not just the power of values to effect change, but the galvanising effect these stories have on people across countries and continents. After reporting about the women in India, I received letters from as far afield as Ghana, Papua New Guinea and Suriname. The story of values is touching because it is also the story of change, progress and hope in an uncertain world that's being radically reshaped by technological, political, business, environmental and social forces.

This brings me back to my roots and the values I grew up with as a Punjabi – which you see in the strength of the women and men. It's the agricultural bread box of India and my ancestors are farmers. They toiled Mother Earth, and were close to her for their provision and sustenance – not only theirs, but for all those around them. Our connection to the earth, the elements, the seasons is fundamental and you see this in their connection to family and community, which will always be very important to us.

Nourish those around you and this leads to a virtuous spiral upwards – with each of us helping and uplifting the other. I saw the women and men in my family be of service to others, and continue to see this daily through my parents – the same way they saw it through their parents, siblings and elders. My paternal great-grandfather (Maha Singh) and grandparents Naranjan Singh and Amar Kaur worked until their departure. My nana ji Harbhajan worked hard until a debilitating accident, and I know my nani Mohinder Kaur worked every day of her life to provide for her family, whilst being an outstanding role model for us, possessing a strong values and faith-based compass. The same is true for each of her siblings – brothers Preet, Dev, and Mohan Singh, and sisters Surinder and Narinder (Nunjo) Kaur. Their parents Piara and Udam are our inspiration. What was important was to be evolving and growing – spiritually and through the principles you give to the next generation. These are the values of my ancestors – growth, contribution, strength, connection, support and love.

Now where do these values come from? Their spiritual foundation over the last 550 years has been based in Sikhi and the aim of chardi kala, which means to think positively through trusting in the spirit, speak positively and act in that sense that is good for all. You see all these principles in the Sikh faith through kirtan (speaking or singing the virtues of the spirit), seva (helping others) and langar (24-hour free community kitchen) and generally sharing what you have from honest labour.

What's interesting from a woman's perspective is how much strength and sacrifice went into this all. Women would fight the battles if required, in all respects – mentally, physically and emotionally – whilst also nourishing, caring and loving. They would exhibit a blend of feminine and masculine energies, and again, this is emphasised in the Sikh qualities and principle of equality.

There are stories of hardship, loss and struggle, many of which I could share. However, Punjabi people are driven by very strong values and rejoice in giving, uplifting and creating a better world for all – Sarbat da Bhalla. For example, my uncle Harren Jhoti has developed a treatment for breast cancer after losing his mother Surinder Nani to cancer, and similarly many members of the family have contributed to the world with such passion and vigour. Whether it be through education, entertainment or the environment, the aim is for this rich land of Punjab and its people to share its voice, commitment and energy with all.

All of the stories contained in this book, in the lives around us, and yours are a reflection of your values. If I spent an hour with you I could probably work out what you spend your time doing. If I spent a week with you I might work out what you like and dislike and what your priorities are. But if I spend quality time with you with an open mind and eyes, for an extended period of time, then I discover what really matters to you and how that affects your behaviour. Those are your values; it is what you are driven by, and once you have articulated them, it helps inform how you would spend your time. Whilst many of us recognise the importance of articulating our values, we may have a difficult time doing so. In my book, *The Values Compass*, I take you through an exercise that could help you, so that you have a tool in your back pocket to navigate you to your best self, effective decisions in line with your values, such that you can lead others and yourself to a more fulfilling and happy life.

My parents, grandparents, ancestors and Sikhi have been fundamental in forming my values. In raising my family I see these values coming to the surface with community, contribution, change, continuity at the core. This is why at home we hold weekly values classes for local children, hold sangat (devotional gatherings), and contribute to the community building around us. Our contribution comes in many forms including service, mentorship, time, investments, connections and inspiration. The aim is to continue what my family taught me – whilst having the courage to apply these values to changing times and create new legacies.

Grandmothers Narinder, Mohinder, Surinder and
Great-grandmothers Bhago and Udam Kaur

Mandeep's sons, Naryan and Sai

The Rai family – today

*My parents on their wedding day with my Mother's siblings –
Kamal, Sukhjeevan, and Gurtej*

Three generations of Mandeep's family

*Mandeep with Arch Bishop Desmond Tutu,
His Holiness the Dalai Lama, and Kofi Annan*

FOURTEEN

The Face of Love
SANTOSH GOYAL

I am very proud of my mother-in-law, and consider her the most courageous woman I know. With perseverance, sacrifice and hard work, she raised a family of entrepreneurs and gave them the tools and the spirit to succeed. The privileged life that I have today is due to her love, commitment and dedication. That is something that I will always be thankful for.

ANITA GOYAL

Every story has a beginning. I suppose this must be mine. My name is Santosh Goyal. My mother, Puran Devi, was born in Daroli Bhai Ki, a village located about fourteen kilometres west of Moga in Moga district, Punjab. According to local folklore, a woman named 'Daroli Bai', who was once a dancer with the Mughals, was rewarded some land for her talent. My father was born in Jagraon, a town and a municipal council, a rural police district and a sub-division of the Ludhiana district in the Indian state of Punjab.

My father was a traditional medicine man and practised Ayurvedic medicine – for a living. Ayurvedic medicine is one of the world's oldest holistic ('whole-body') healing systems. It was developed more than 3,000 years ago in India. It is based on the belief that health and wellness depend on a delicate balance between the mind, body and spirit. I believe in Ayurveda, as it saved me from having a medical hysterectomy. Those were good years. But, in his final days, my father got very sick. His voice suffered; after a while, his hands and feet stopped moving. It was Parkinson's.

In the early days, my dynamic father, Muni Lal, was part of Arya Samaj, which teaches a spiritual way of living with a universal message of peace and happiness. It was founded by Maharishi Swami Dayanand Saraswati on 10 April 1875 in Mumbai, India. It teaches love, justice and righteousness towards all, irrespective of race, caste or creed. Members of the Arya Samaj believe in one God and reject the worship of idols. A prominent freedom fighter, Lala Lajpat Rai was devoted to Arya Samaj, and many noble men were part of this movement. The teachings helped to bring equality to women, especially women who were widowed. This new way of thinking at that time influenced the conversations and way of thinking of the family.

My parents married in 1925 in Punjab, where two years later my eldest brother, Rajinder, was born. He sadly passed away at the age of eighteen. In 1928, my father went to Kenya in the pursuit of a better life for us all and my mother joined him with her firstborn two years later. It was in Mombasa (Kenya) that my older sister, Kuldeep Kanta, was born in 1931. My entrance into the world came shortly after in 1933. My dear brother Braham Rattan was born in 1935. Braham Rattan has always had a profound influence in my family and helped my husband and I create a great vision for our future. He has always been a high achiever and would study late into the night under candlelight with all the family sleeping beside him in one room.

Life was harsh for us in Kenya, and my father decided to return to India in 1938. I was only five years old at the time. We went to live in Jagraon in Punjab where we remained until I was fifteen years old. My two younger brothers, Bhisham Dev and Satpal, were born in Jagraon.

Growing up was so different to how it is now, as I never went to school and didn't receive a formal education. My life experience is my education. We lived in India during the Partition of India in 1947, and it was a time that many girls in Punjab were not being sent out, purely for our safety. I never saw anything bad happen, not with my own eyes, but the stories were impossible to ignore. The rumours were that many people had been robbed. Our people were scared. It was the Pakistanis and Muslims, and the Punjabi and Sikh. They were fighting when I left. The way the world is now, there is still so much conflict.

Our street was quite big, but the girls remained indoors helping the other women with household chores. In 1945, my sister's marriage was arranged to a man from Burma who was twelve years older than her. People were keen to marry their daughters off at a young age and that was my sister's fate. It was in 1948 that my father was in correspondence with a friend in Kenya and this good friend paid for the passage of six people to travel. I returned to Kenya on a ship at the age of fifteen where I was promised to a man, and I recall that he was discouraged from coming to see me as everyone was concerned that I would decline him. It's a funny thing as everyone assumed I would say no to marriage as my skin was very fair and my husband was of a darker complexion! My wedding day was very simple: I washed my hair, tied it into a high bun, wore no makeup and was dressed in a cream-coloured saree. I was a married woman with many responsibilities at the tender age of seventeen; it was 1950. My husband, Hemraj Goyal, was a simple, helpful and kind man. Hemraj came from India to Nairobi to work and marry. Five of my children were born in Kenya. If things had been different, we might still be there.

It was during the time we lived in Nairobi that my eldest son fell ill. We didn't exactly know what was wrong with Bharat Bhushan; to this day I couldn't tell you, but my brother Braham Rattan describes it as rheumatic fever. We searched for treatment. I was so desperate for a cure that I took my son to Mombasa. I remember that long train journey with my son; it's still so fresh in my mind. We had friends in Mombasa, and they helped us get him admitted to hospital where the doctors examined him and, without hesitation, declared that there wasn't much they could do. I stayed with my son for many months whilst my mother took care of my other children in Nairobi. Sadly, there wasn't any progress. At that time, I found the strength within me, through all my pain, not to share my sorrow with anyone. Eventually, after much discussion with the family we reached a decision to take him to India with my other children, Sulakshana, Pratibha, Vidya Bhushan and Ranjana.

When we were preparing to move in 1963, my husband was worried about whether I would be able to cope in India. He would ask me, "Will you cover your head, *khund kadegi*, in India? In Kenya we have servants. Will you be able to live without servants in India? Here you get help even if you need a spoon, what will you do in India?" I told him not to worry, I wouldn't ask for anything. I kept my word. When we moved to India, I did every possible kind of work, from A to Z. I even covered my head in the house, *khund kadeya*. I did all sorts of housework. I fetched the water; I took care of our two cows; I cooked and I cleaned as well as giving birth to four more children.

We had two cows. I would roll and pat their dung into bricks and we used that for the fire, so we could cook. On the rooftop, I added the dirt for the roof, the way you would add plaster to a rooftop here. My husband said we could hire people, but I said, "No, I can do it." And I did. I did all the work, and I did it happily. I never complained or regretted coming to India. I just carried on. I never felt sadness. I loved the work that came with living in India. I never slept during the day, did not even so much as rest. I remember I used to milk the cows and send milk to my brothers' families. I never cheated them by sending them less milk; I kept it equal and fair for all our families. I never felt that I was doing more work than anyone else.

We had moved to India to find treatment for my eldest son. We tried many things, but unfortunately, he never got any better. One day, he just slipped away. He was only eighteen. I still wonder if he might have survived had we come to England instead of India. We wanted him to get better, but that never happened. When he passed away, I was devastated and heartbroken. He was always so considerate and thoughtful. I remember when he used to worry about whether we would have enough money to marry off his four sisters at the time we were in India. We had started a small business but it never took off, and then my son died. It was time for us to leave India.

After the death of my son in 1969, my brother Rattan encouraged us to come to the United Kingdom. He said it was time to close our small business and get our passports ready to go to London with my children including my newborn baby girl who was born shortly after my son died. Our passports had long expired; we never bothered to keep them up to date. I had to have a marriage certificate in order to do this and I didn't have one! We had a real challenge with the British Embassy to get my passport; I was refused twice. Eventually we began our arrangements and my husband was the first to leave. He went back to Africa where he made further provisions and then came to London via Paris. When he arrived in London, he rented a room to live in and then he prepared to bring all of us over from India. He began working for the local buses and found a three-bedroom house for us to rent in Romford.

When we were living in Nairobi, we had originally planned to move to the UK, not to India, to get treatment for my son. But, people in Nairobi told us, "In England, there is so much snow, there's not enough food." We were alarmed. How could we move somewhere when there was freezing weather and no food? We got scared and instead of moving to England we went to India. When we finally did arrive in England, we laughed at how wrong people had been. Sure, it is cold in England, but it's not unbearable, and of course, there is enough food. You shouldn't always believe what people tell you, I suppose.

We lived for many months in that rented house in Romford. Then we got an offer to rent a council house in Basildon at Roodegate, so we moved there. At that time, the council practically gave you a house for free when you had as many children as we had; one had passed away, but we still had eight children. The council even gave us spending money. We rented there for a few months and then were offered the opportunity to buy the house, so we bought it. It became ours! We still own it; it's in Basildon.

I didn't speak English when I arrived in London. Where would I have learned English from? Even Vidya, my eldest son, didn't speak much English when we first came here, but he picked it up and quickly learned how to work in, and navigate around, London. He would take the older children like Sulakshana and Pratibha to the city and he set them up with jobs. They couldn't speak much English either, and they were afraid they'd get lost in the city. But Vidya was like a father figure to them; he would drop them off and pick them up from work so they didn't get lost. He would also help us with the shopping. I was afraid to go shopping in the markets. What if someone grabbed me? What if someone kidnapped the children? I don't know why I was afraid, but I was.

Vidya showed us how to go shopping. He taught us how to take our time and walk through all the aisles, with our trolley in tow. He was very sharp and completely fearless. My husband was working day and night, so it was Vidya who helped me and the family to learn how to live here in England.

We learned that electricity was cheaper in the mornings, so we had a daily routine: one person had to wake up early and turn the geezer (boiler) on to warm the water. Everyone had to shower, one after the next. By 9am every morning, even on weekends, the entire family had bathed, eaten breakfast and drunk *chai*. We would all be free by 9am, even on Sundays. It was a smooth process, there was never any fighting or bad attitude; we all lived together very happily. The children were never fussy about food, for instance. I could make anything – *daal, subji*, anything – and they would eat it, happily. I never asked them what I should make, and no one ever complained about what I'd cook.

Our salary at that time was about £20 unless you worked overtime. But things weren't so expensive, then. You could fill up your shopping trolley for about £4 or £5 in those days – butter only cost ten pence. We rented a television set. No one bought TVs then, everyone rented them. It cost about fifty pence per week. Vidya had arranged some work for me from London; I would sew flowers from cloth that could be attached to shoes. I would get about £4 or £5 for sewing those and that covered the cost of our weekly grocery shop. Nowadays, you'd think what can £5 buy? But then it could buy a lot! We saved our money from doing all these odd jobs and collected enough to buy the house.

I started working at a factory in Billericay while we lived in that house. My job was to help pack flowerpots into boxes at the factory. I would start work at 4pm and return home after 11pm. I had to walk and then take a bus to get to the factory and back; it would always be dark by the time I made my way home. At night, it would take me a full hour to get home. In those days, though, I didn't feel any fear about being out so late.

Eventually, we bought a shop in Romford, a newsagent that I would run with my eldest son, Vidya. We moved there and lived above the shop. There were three bedrooms in that place and a sitting room downstairs next to the shop. The shop was quite small when we bought it, but we extended it and the business really took off! When we were buying it, my husband was hesitant. It took quite a bit of convincing. He thought the shop was too small and that nothing would come of it. But Vidya ran it so well, it just took off.

Then, we sold the shop and bought another one, and then one more in Laindon, and one more in Southend. We bought and sold many shops, but it all started with one. My eldest daughter, Sulakshana, was born in 1951 in Nairobi. She was a beautiful soul who always thought of others before herself. Sulakshana helped run the shops in the early days, but we lost her in her battle with breast cancer in her late thirties, sparking another devastating time for me and the family. I often think about her and miss her so much.

We eventually moved to Basildon where we all lived together in one house; we stayed very close. Everything was cooked in the house. We go out to restaurants now, but back then we never did; we cooked everything in the house – two full meals a day and then lunch was at the shops. I get so much happiness when the whole family gets together, there's nothing better. I only wish that my eldest son and daughter were still alive today in my old age.

We didn't have much choice when we were younger. We didn't have opportunities to travel and go on holidays. We found so much happiness just being together. Even now, I don't regret that I didn't travel or see the world, because I spent all my time with my children and running the house.

I didn't know much when I was younger. As a young girl growing up in Punjab and Nairobi, I wasn't exposed to that ambitious kind of learning. I sometimes wonder what I could have become if I had an education. I could have learned, I could have studied, I could have been somebody important. Even now at this age, I might be tired, but if someone is talking about something interesting, something positive, I stay awake and make the effort to listen because I know I can learn from them. I am proud that my children have worked so hard in their lives and have a great entrepreneurial spirit, which I think started when they were involved in the businesses from a young age. It has helped them to learn so much in life and they are successful in their own way; each and every one of my children is unique and different in their own way. I am surrounded by a huge family and they all care for my every need. I see this more when my health deteriorates and they all come together to be around me; I know I am blessed. I am also a great-grandmother now and so happy that I have lived to see my great-grandson grow up.

Sometimes, I think that in my next life, no matter if I come back as a man or a woman, I won't want to get married. Instead, I want to dedicate my whole life to doing good. I want to do something in charity. Even now, I feel restless, I just want to help and do something good. Before, I had issues with my health. But even earlier in my life, I wanted to work to earn and gather up some money with my own hands to give away to charity. When I pray, I ask for good health so that I can be strong enough to help someone in need. I don't need anything for myself, I just want to feel like I can help someone – anyone, a family member, a stranger, anyone. I just want to do *seva* (a

Sanskrit word meaning 'selfless service' or work performed without any thought of reward or repayment). In ancient India, *seva* was believed to help one's spiritual growth and at the same time contribute to the improvement of a community. I don't have any desire to travel or go on holiday or go shopping. I have enjoyed all the places I've been, I've enjoyed being with my children and my family. My life has been full and I have lived it well.

When my youngest son, Avnish, set up the Hemraj Goyal Foundation in memory of my late husband in 2010, I was so proud that his legacy continues. His name lives on in all the different charities that are supported. So many people hear his name through the foundation and that makes me feel special. My grandchildren have so many opportunities to achieve so many things in this country. My own children have achieved so much; even though we lived through financial hardship in the 1970s and '80s, it all worked out well in the end.

Anita Goyal, Santosh Goyal and Avnish Goyal
(founder of Hallmark Care Homes)

Mataji (centre) with all her grandchildren

Santosh with her two children, her husband Hemraj Goyal,
and brothers Braham Rattan, Satpal and Bhisham

Prince Philip, Duke of Edinburgh, Parmjit Rai, Santosh Goyal
and Avnish Goyal at Buckingham Palace

Santosh with her grandchildren fundraising for the charity LILY
Against Human Trafficking at the Battle of Bollywood
dance competition in London

Santosh Goyal with her daughter-in-law Anita

ACKNOWLEDGEMENTS

I never thought that I could ever write a book until I started. It all starts with a thought and the first few words. I thank my co-author, Aastha K Singhania, for her hard work, commitment and dedication in making this book come to life. Her ideas, support and suggestions have been pivotal in shaping the stories and supporting the interviews and being there on this incredible journey. Together we have bonded, learnt so much and created some magical memories that will be the foundation for many more inspirational projects.

The stories have steered the direction of the book, and each and every woman has given us a precious gift: messages of their life experience that has broadened our experience, awareness, understanding and perspective. My heartfelt gratitude towards these magnificent women: Kalbir Bains, Mani K Bajwa, Rita Chowdhry, Lady Kishwar Desai, Santosh Goyal, Dr Kamel Hothi OBE, Rajni Kaul, Seema Malhotra MP, Raj Nayyar, Lady Mohini Kent Noon, Dr Mandeep Rai, Parmjit Rai, Sarita Sabharwal, Kuljit Sharma and Baroness Sandip Verma. I have spent the last year totally absorbed with each and every story and feel that we have a very special connection now.

I would like to thank Francesca Douglas for the wonderful support in strengthening the stories and being my first reader. I am so grateful for the time, effort and passion that you have spent on taking this book to the publishers.

I am grateful to my beautiful, kind mother, Parmjit Rai, for having faith in me and encouraging me to complete my first book.

My heartfelt gratitude towards my amazing husband for always trusting me with my vision and challenging me to take this book to the finishing line. I wouldn't have been able to complete this project without Avnish's kindness, patience and enthusiasm.

THE AUTHORS

Anita Goyal

Anita Goyal is currently the CEO and a trustee of the Hemraj Goyal Foundation and the Hallmark Care Homes Foundation. She is a patron of Binti International and Honorary Chair of the FGM Appeal for Barnardo's. She is an award-winning philanthropist and community champion. Anita completed a BSc in Biomedical Materials Science and Engineering at Queen Mary College, London. Her passion for teaching led her to become a science teacher, advancing to Head of Science and then progressing to Assistant Head Teacher of Inclusion. Anita has completed an MA in Special and Inclusive Education at the Institute of Education and UCL. She is the co-founder of Ultimate You where she designs educational seminars for business, leadership, life and relationships with her husband, Avnish Goyal (an award-winning entrepreneur). Under the family foundation, Anita has launched People of the World as a platform for investing in the personal development and empowerment of all people from diverse backgrounds. She is passionate about making a difference and believes in doing everything with passion and purpose.

Aastha Kapoor Singhania

Aastha K Singhania is currently working as a co-manager of First Class Learning Hendon, Hampstead and Wood Green, an after-class tutorial centre. Aastha completed her BA (Hons) in English from St Bede's College, Shimla (Himachal Pradesh University) with a gold medal, securing the first position all over the state. She then went on to work as an in-house reporter at NDTV New Delhi for almost a year and gained experience in reporting, editing and scriptwriting with her ten-month training at the channel's media institute. Aastha also has a Master's degree in Literature from King's College London, studying literary years from 1850 to Post-Modernity, extensively studying the Mahabharata and its visual depiction. Aastha is passionate about writing stories that can make a difference and inspire others to become what they have always dreamt of.

THE HEMRAJ GOYAL FOUNDATION

Hemraj Goyal joined the Dev Samaj community in the 1960s whilst living in Moga, Punjab. The Dev Samaj (a unique movement) was founded in 1887 by Bhagwan Dev Atma. Dev Samaj took positive steps to build a social structure where women could enjoy a respectable position, free from gender bias. The organisation promotes equal rights and status to women with men while adopting many social reforms such as recognition of a girl child, monogamy, widow remarriage and dowryless marriages. The Dev Samaj considers women's education as a core essential for their social, moral and spiritual upliftment. The founder of Dev Samaj realised that the future of women lay in education. Education alone could open opportunities of enlightenment and independence for women. He wanted to regenerate mankind and transform society through the education of women. This influenced and shaped Hemraj's thinking and he carried the photo of Bhagwan Dev Atma everywhere he went whilst living in the UK. This reminded him of the commitment he had towards cultivating harmonious relationships with the four kingdoms – the Kingdom of the Inanimate, the Kingdom of Vegetation, the Kingdom of Animals and the Kingdom of Human Beings – through feelings of respect, appreciation and gratitude.

The Hemraj Goyal Foundation was founded in 2010 by Avnish Goyal, in honour of Hemraj Goyal who moved his family to the UK with a vision of a better life.

Since establishing the charity in his memory, the family of Hemraj Goyal have dedicated time, finances and resources to helping women and children across the globe, through a series of charity partnerships and projects. The vision that Hemraj Goyal had for a better world has extended to his children, his grandchildren and beyond, all of whom are true advocates for next-generation philanthropy and engaging young people in charitable activity.

The growth of the foundation over the last nine years has led to HGF being an established charity, with ongoing partnerships alongside the likes of Barnardo's, the Outward Bound Trust, British Asian Trust, Binti International, Child Action, the Cherie Blair Foundation and many more.

HGF is passionate about building a sustainable future for the children and women of today. It distributes funds to organisations with a clear vision, a vision for a world where children have the right to education, are free from suffering and abuse, women's rights are empowered and children with disabilities are offered a chance to fulfil their potential.

HGF proudly supports promotion of good relations and community cohesion between all faith groups, helping to narrow gaps in identified communities.